A THEOLOGY
OF WISDOM

A THEOLOGY
OF WISDOM

A Study in St. Thomas

Kieran Conley, O.S.B.

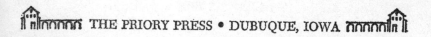 THE PRIORY PRESS • DUBUQUE, IOWA

Revisor Ordinis: Marcianus Strange, O.S.B., S.S.L., S.T.L.

Imprimi potest: Bonaventura Knaebel, O.S.B., Abbas

Nihil obstat: Thomas C. Donlan, O.P., S.T.Lr., S.T.D., Censor Librorum

Imprimatur: Iacobus I. Byrne, S.T.D., Archiepiscopus Dubuquensis, die 7a Martii, 1963

First Printing

Library of Congress Card No. 63-12430

To My
Mother and Father

INTRODUCTION

"Where is the wisdom we have lost in knowledge?"[1] To a modern world no longer in quest of ultimates, too often accepting the pragmatic for the true, enamored more of the *how* than of the *why*, such a question has no meaning. The word, *wisdom*, for the twentieth-century mind can suggest little more than a gossamer of abstractions, floating hopelessly out of contact with the dynamic world of reality in which we find ourselves. Wisdom has lost not only its real, but also its intentional, existence. We simply are not interested.

If wisdom is a stranger to contemporary minds, it was not so to more ancient ones. To the worlds of Plato and Aristotle, of Solomon and St. Paul, of St. Augustine and St. Thomas—to these worlds, wisdom was not a conceptual outcast, unknown and unwelcome; it was the heart of the matter. Such a sweep through pagan, Judaic, and Christian antiquity must obviously transcend a univocal conception of wisdom. It finds its justification only in a consideration of wisdom as analogous, as open to diverse realizations which retain a common value. The scope of the present study will be to present these diverse realizations of wisdom, not precisely as conceived by each of the individuals named above, though their respective positions will be referred to briefly, but rather as discovered in the letter and the spirit

[1] T. S. Eliot, "The Rock," *Collected Poems* (New York: Harcourt, Brace & Co., 1934), p. 179.

of St. Thomas Aquinas, who more significantly than any other writer has distinguished the different wisdoms. It is hoped that the forbidding caricature of wisdom, as a collection of meaningless abstractions out of contact with our existential world, may be made to appear as the caricature it is, and that for us, too, wisdom must be the heart of the matter.

In order to see the thought of St. Thomas in context, there is a minimum of historical background necessary, at least to understand some of the influences which helped to shape his thought on wisdom. The word, minimum, is important, because although a purely historical study of the problem would be possible and extremely valuable, the present work must content itself with but a modicum of what is purely history. Since it is primarily a speculative essay, a complete historical treatment of the subject will be left to specialists, and the background presented here will be taken largely from secondary sources.[2]

Before concluding this introduction, the author wishes to express his gratitude, first of all, to the Reverend Jean-Hervé Nicolas, O.P., for his generous advice and criticism which proved extremely helpful throughout the development of the book. He is indebted also to Monsignor Charles Journet who followed the work in progress and whose inspiration and encouragement lightened considerably the dual burden of research and writing. Lastly, sincere thanks are extended to the Reverends Basil Mattingly, O.S.B., Cornelius Williams, O.P., William A. Wallace, O.P., Gregory Baum, O.S.A., and William H. Wallaik for their critical observations and suggestions, theological as well as literary. To all these individuals the author is deeply grateful for

[2]While the importance of history in doctrinal study cannot be minimized, there are valid reasons for limiting the extent of historical investigation in a speculative study. One of those reasons is mentioned by a contemporary theologian, and is not without application to the present work: "Il est fréquent de voir annoncer des ouvrages à la fois positifs et spéculatifs. Mais . . . il est excessivement rare que l'auteur donne l'impression d'être parfaitement chez lui dans l'une et l'autre partie de son oeuvre." R. Gagnebet, O.P., "Le problème actuel de la théologie et la science aristotélicienne," *Divus Thomas Piacenza*, 20 (1943), pp. 261-62.

their help and for what is more important, their friendship. Whatever there may be of value in the work is due in large measure to their suggestions—its shortcomings, however, are the unenviable responsibility of the writer.

For the rest, the author proposes to pronounce no last words and only hopes that in some measure his work might serve toward a theology of wisdom.

❖ ❖ ❖

An explanation regarding the method of citation may be helpful to those unfamiliar with the short-title system. From the reader's point of view there is but one wholly satisfactory method of citing the works of other authors—it is to give complete information each time any reference is made. This would automatically eliminate the annoying search for an elusive *opus citatum*. While this ideal method is prohibitive, a shortened version of multiple citation—without the plaguing *op. cit.*—shall be adopted. Under this short-title system complete information is presented only the first time a work appears in the footnotes. In subsequent citations the title of the work referred to is given in shortened form, together with the necessary page or pages. If the full reference is not immediately recalled, the reader can readily find it presented in the bibliography at the end of the book.

CONTENTS

Contents

I

HISTORICAL CONSIDERATION

OF WISDOM

If St. Thomas is to be the light of our study, the major historical currents to be considered seem reducible to three: 1) the pagan sources of Greek philosophy, represented by Plato and, above all, by Aristotle; 2) the Judaic mind as portrayed in the sapiential books of the Old Testament; and 3) the Christian tradition from St. Paul in the New Testament, through St. Augustine among the Fathers, to the scholastics prior to St. Thomas himself. The historical sketch presented here will follow that pattern with brief expositions made of Greek, Judaic, New Testament, and Augustinian wisdom. The transition from St. Augustine to the thirteenth century and St. Thomas will conclude the history outline and set the stage for the speculative study that follows.

I. WISDOM IN GREEK PHILOSOPHY[1]

A. PRE-ARISTOTELIAN THOUGHT

In the Hellenic world before the golden age of the Academy and the Lyceum, wisdom (σοφία) enjoyed a varied life. The Greek mind attributed wisdom variously to those possessing a

---

[1]Cf. among secondary sources: A. J. Festugière, *Contemplation et vie contemplative selon Platon* (Paris: Vrin, 1936); *The Great Ideas—a Syntopicon of the Great Books of the Western World*, ed., M. Adler (London: Encyclopedia Britannica Ltd., 1952); T. Heath, O.P., *Aristotelian Influence*

1

savoir-vivre in general, to the world of artistic excellence, to religious men respecting the gods; even the dialectic of the sophists was thought to be wisdom.[2] Before Socrates, Plato, and Aristotle gave to Greek wisdom its philosophical overtones, Homer and Sophocles, Phidias and Policlitus were the heroes of wisdom.[3] With poets and dramatists, sculptors and architects as the "wise men" of Greek culture, the protean perfection of σοφία added sophistry as one of its realizations. It was against this latter conception that Socrates reacted, affirming that true wisdom is nothing else but that supreme perfection of the soul which is knowledge of self and of one's ignorance.[4] But he would not call any man wise, a name reserved, as he thought, to God alone; rather, Socrates echoed the humble answer of Pythagoras: men can be only philosophers (φιλόσοφοι), *lovers of wisdom.*[5]

In the tradition of Socrates and Plato σοφία (wisdom) becomes almost identified with φρόνησις (prudence), as a unified view of ends and means, resulting from an examination of the various arts (τέχναι). Here, in the ordering proper to τέχνη, the maxim, *sapientis est ordinare,* finds its source.[6] In the conception of Plato the function of directing conduct is joined to the contemplation of the truth; the clear distinction made

---

in *Thomistic Wisdom: a Comparative Study* (Washington: Cath. Univ. Press, 1956); J. Hirschberger, "Quod sit officium sapientis," *Philosophisches Jahrbuch,* 53 (1940) 30-44; J. Lenz, "Thomistische Philosophie als Lebensweisheit," *Pastor Bonus,* 49 (1939-40) 323-37; J. Maritain, "Science et sagesse," *Nova et Vetera,* 9 (1934) 389-407; *Id., Science et sagesse* (Paris: Labergerie, 1936); M. D. Philippe, O.P., *Initiation à la philosophie d'Aristote* (Paris: La Colombe, 1956); *Id.,* "Nature de l'acte de contemplation philosophique dans la perspective des principes d'Aristote," *Revue thomiste,* 49 (1949) 525-41; *Id.,* "La sagesse selon Aristote," *Nova et Vetera,* 20 (1945) 325-74.

[2] Cf. M. D. Philippe, "La Sagesse," p. 326.

[3] Cf. F. Prat, S.J., *La théologie de St. Paul* (Paris: Beauchesne, 1912), I, 128. See also Aristotle, *Nicomachean Ethics,* Bk. VI, chap. 7 (1141 a 9 ff.).

[4] Cf. M. D. Philippe, "La sagesse," p. 326.

[5] Cf. *Syntopicon,* II, 1105. Worth noting here is the remarkable bibliography on *wisdom* presented in this work, II, 1110-16. Cf. also St. Thomas, *In I Meta.,* lect. 3, no. 56.

[6] Cf. Hirschberger, "Quod sit officium," pp. 33-34. See also Lenz, "Thomistische Philosophie," p. 324, and *Syntopicon,* II, 1103, 1107.

between speculative and practical is a later development of Aristotle and has little in common with Platonic wisdom. For Plato, the reign of reason over all the passions and activities led to the contemplation of the beautiful, and although its most proper act remained contemplation, σοφία was identified also with the whole complex movement towards contemplation.[7] The term of that movement held the secret of human happiness, realized in contemplation. It was not simply an intuition of essences or first principles, nor even the characteristic return of science to principles whose virtuality has been realized; for Plato, contemplation was rather "a sentiment of presence, a contact with Being seized in its very existence."[8]

The richness of this Platonic conception deserves to be developed more fully. However, Plato failed to distinguish sufficiently between the speculative and the practical, and for St. Thomas, this distinction is fundamental. Consequently, within the Greek tradition, it is Aristotle who must receive most of our attention.

B. THE DOCTRINE OF ARISTOTLE

The mature thought of Aristotle on the nature of wisdom is presented first in the sixth book of the *Nicomachean Ethics* and later, in book one of his *Metaphysics*. According to some authors, the clear distinction, found in these sources, between the speculative and practical intellect, and therefore between wisdom and prudence, represents a change from his position in the earlier *Eudaemonean Ethics*.[9] Whether or not Aristotle

---

[7]Cf. M. D. Philippe, "La sagesse," p. 327.

[8]Festugière, *Contemplation*, p. 5. "Etre heureux, c'est imiter Dieu, Mesure Souveraine. Mais l'imiter, c'est le connaître et cette connaissance est contemplation." *Ibid.*, p. 8.

[9]Cf. Festugière, *Contemplation*, p. 18. See also Hirschberger, "Quod sit officium," p. 36. The *Syntopicon* simply mentions that although Aristotle sometimes fails to divide wisdom into speculative and practical, he seldom overlooks that separation, cf. II, 1104. Chapters one and four of Book One of the *Eudaemonean Ethics* do seem to justify the opinion, for Aristotle there links prudence (φρόνησις) with contemplation (θεωρία ἡ περὶ τὴν ἀλήθειαν) in the "philosophical life," as distinguished from the virtuous and pleasurable lives.

did align himself more closely with Plato in the earlier work is not vital to the discussion here, for his later writings have left us the definitive Aristotelian concept of wisdom.

1. In the *Nicomachean Ethics* wisdom is enumerated twice among the five intellectual virtues, as philosophical and as practical.[10] Philosophical wisdom is presented later as the "most finished of the forms of knowledge. It follows that the wise man must not only know what follows from first principles, but must also possess truth about the first principles. Therefore wisdom must be intuitive reason (understanding) combined with scientific knowledge—scientific knowledge of the highest objects . . ."[11] From this necessary contact with highest objects Aristotle argues to exclude practical wisdom (here political, but further distinguished in chapter eight) as the best kind of knowledge, which must concern the things that are highest by nature. This latter knowledge, philosophical wisdom, is attributed to Anaxagoras, Thales, and men like them "when we see them ignorant of what is to their own advantage . . . they know things that are remarkable, admirable, difficult and divine, but useless."[12] It seems curious that throughout chapters three to seven, Aristotle does not once mention explicitly the word, *cause,* although when he speaks of demonstration, it is certainly implicit. Wisdom as knowledge of "highest causes" must await the exposition in book one of the *Metaphysics* to be made explicit. What remains clear in the treatment of the intellectual virtues in the *Ethics* is the definitive departure from the Socratic-Platonic linking of speculative and practical. Wisdom, in the fullest sense, is for Aristotle only speculative.

2. Presupposing what he had written in the *Ethics,* Aristotle begins in the *Metaphysics* an investigation of "the causes and principles, the knowledge of which is wisdom."[13] He

[10]Bk. VI, chap. 3 (1139 b 17).
[11]*Ibid.,* chap. 7 (1141 a 16-18).
[12]*Ibid.,* (1141 b 5-7).
[13]Bk. I, chap. 2 (982 a 6). The analysis that follows is paraphrased from Aristotle's thought here in chapter two.

examines several characteristics common to the accepted notion of what and how a wise man must know and from this analysis establishes the criterion by which he will judge first philosophy to be wisdom. First among the qualifications is that the wise man be omniscient; not, of course, that he know everything in detail, but that the light in which he views all things be universal enough to illumine all reality. Secondly, he must know difficult things beyond the powers of the ordinary mind. Thirdly, his knowledge must be certain, a knowledge through causes. This, in turn, qualifies the wise man as a teacher, the fourth quality in the composite of opinion studied by Aristotle. Fifthly, wisdom cannot be something pragmatic; it is a knowledge sought disinterestedly, for its own sake, and is, therefore, purely speculative. Finally, as "the most finished form of knowledge," wisdom is supreme. It is subordinated to no other; rather, it is the wise man who must order, the less wise must obey him.[14]

For Aristotle, the test of omniscience is met by a knowledge that is most universal, and this character of universality suggests, at the same time, the difficulty associated with objects furthest removed from the immediacy of sense experience. While certitude in any science depends upon its contact with first principles, that contact as causal makes the science instructive. Moreover, the first principles and causes themselves are most knowable and therefore invite a disinterested search of knowledge for its own sake. Finally, a science's prerogative to order presupposes not a simple awareness of cause, but of final cause, of end, of good. "Judged by all the tests we have mentioned, then, the name in question (wisdom) falls to the same science; this must be a science that investigates the first principles and causes; for the good, i.e., the end, is one of the causes."[15]

[14]Aristotle's most famous commentator summarizes the six characteristics of the wise man in the following manner: "Ille sapiens dicatur, qui scit omnia etiam difficilia per certitudinem et causam, ipsum scire propter se quaerens, alios ordinans et persuadens." St. Thomas, *In I Meta.*, lect. 2, no. 43.

[15]Aristotle, *Metaphysics*, Bk. I, chap. 2 (982 b 7-10).

A theology of wisdom

In this manner Aristotle introduces his metaphysics, the highest of the sciences, possessing a name proper to itself, *wisdom*. "All men by nature desire to know,"[16] and from this radical wonder the mind rises ultimately to searching ultimates. Entering here the rarefied atmosphere of the divine, it breathes the air of first principles and causes—it has arrived at the summit of human knowledge, enjoying the universality, the profundity, the certitude, the communicability, the desirableness and the nobility proper to wisdom.

Aristotle's conception of wisdom certainly means something more than simply that first contact with highest causes. The possession of such a vantage point, while offering the repose of having arrived, presupposes the ascent and, at the same time, confers upon the metaphysician certain prerogatives of judgment. All of this implies a plurality of functions proper to wisdom. The repose is contemplative, the prior ascent, strictly scientific, while the privileged judgment suggests the other sapiential functions concerned with principles and inferiors.[17]

If, for Aristotle, wisdom is knowledge of ultimate cause, then metaphysics remains but an inchoative wisdom until it has demonstrated the existence of God. Properly speaking, therefore, in the order of generation the scientific or demonstrative function is prior to wisdom's contemplative act which must, as we shall see later, concern God. It is also true that the evaluation and defense of first principles, whose foundation is being, demand a profound understanding of that concept, and this can be realized only in the scientific investigation of being's principles and causes. But although a certain priority can thus be defended among these functions of Aristotelian wisdom, the

[16]*Ibid.*, chap. 1 (980 a 21).

[17]The phrase, *strictly scientific*, introduces a problem which will be discussed more thoroughly later, in the doctrinal section of the work. Since wisdom is a certain (quaedam) science, the relationship between the two notions is difficult to precise and has been the subject of controversy. Here the words, *strictly scientific*, denote simply demonstration, that operation of the mind essential to every science.

importance of their close interrelation and interpenetration should not be minimized.

Obviously, to present a fully elaborated structure of Aristotle's metaphysics is beyond the scope of this initial chapter. Since St. Thomas conceives the nature of metaphysics in rather strict dependence upon Aristotle, the discussion of wisdom's scientific, judicative-defensive, and contemplative functions will be reserved to the following chapter.[18]

*　*　*

The wisdom of Greece represents the high-point of pagan culture in the west.[19] A modern author places it significantly in the middle between two other wisdoms, both of which find their meaning in salvation and deliverance.[20] In the oriental world Hindu wisdom represents the *ascent* to conquer salvation by purely human effort, tendentially a movement toward pure negation, while in the Jewish world of the Old Testament, the wisdom of salvation has an opposite character. It is the *descent* of Eternal Wisdom, gratuitously given and received in humility. Between these two poles, one a natural mystique, the other totally supernatural, Hellenic wisdom seeks to create the *perfectum opus rationis,* a wisdom of man, of reason. Certainly, the philosophical heritage left to western civilization by that culture is something for which we must be very grateful, and we shall see later its profound influence on Christian thought; however, the wisdom of Greece remained incomplete at its summit. Even Aristotle failed to see clearly the oneness (unicity) of God, a view absolutely essential for a complete wisdom. And one might reasonably conclude that the obscurity shrouding an

[18]Regarding Aristotle's thought, see especially the studies of M. D. Philippe, cited above in note 1.

[19]The vast field of oriental thought on wisdom has purposely been left out of the historical development leading to the thirteenth century. First of all, it exercised no influence on the thought of St. Thomas; and secondly, it represents so vast a tradition with myriad nuances in thought and expression, that it would be impossible to treat it here in the manner it deserves.

[20]Maritain, *Science et saggesse,* pp. 22-35. See also by the same author the article, "Science et sagesse," *Nova et Vetera,* 9 (1934) 389-407.

intellectual world without revelation deprived Greek wisdom of its perfect completion.

II. Wisdom in Sacred Scripture

Leaving, for the moment, the pagan world of ancient Greece, our brief historical conspectus looks of necessity to the world of Jewish and Christian revelation. Because the thirteenth century had a profound respect for the tradition of revealed religion, any attempt to understand the currents which influenced its intellectual life must necessarily involve a study of sacred scripture. The problem is reduced to this: To what extent did the revealed concept of wisdom, which held a unique position in the attention of the sacred writers, influence St. Thomas's doctrine on wisdom? But to answer this question, we must first know what revelation tells us about wisdom. This is our present concern.

A. WISDOM IN THE OLD TESTAMENT[21]

In the sapiential literature of the Jewish world two distinct currents of thought are noticeable. From the secular, aristocratic milieu of the surrounding cultures Israel inherited an interest in a wisdom born of good sense, experience and observation, something essentially rational and practical. The so-called wisdom schools developed in this tradition, dedicated as they were to teaching the rules for a happy, successful life. At the same

[21]Cf. the following works: W. Baumgartner, *Israëlitische und Altorientalische Weisheit*, Sammlung Gemeinverständlicher Vorträge, No. 166 (Tübingen, 1933); B. Botte, O.S.B., "La sagesse dans les livres sapientiaux," *Revue des sciences philosophiques et théologiques*, 19 (1930) 83-94; H. Duesberg, O.S.B., *Les scribes inspirés*, Introduction aux livres sapientiaux de la Bible (Paris: Desclée de Brouwer, 1939); R. E. Murphy, O. Carm., *Seven Books of Wisdom* (Milwaukee: Bruce, 1960); C. Spicq, O.P., "La vertu de prudence dans l'ancien Testament," *Revue biblique*, 42 (1933) 187-210; P. Van Imschoot, "Sagesse et esprit dans l'ancien Testament," *Revue biblique*, 47 (1938) 23-49; and the following studies in *Wisdom in Israel and the Ancient Near East*, eds., M. Noth & D. W. Thomas (Leiden: Brill, 1955): P. DeBoer, "The Counsellor"; J. Lindblom, "Wisdom in the Old Testament Prophets"; S. Mowinckel, "Psalms and Wisdom"; and N. Porteous, "Royal Wisdom."

time, within the more immediately religious context of Jewish cult and culture, another wisdom is discernible. Born of faith, it is a gift of God, sought in prayer and bestowed upon men by a special grace. Suggesting first a personification of a divine attribute and later being assimilated more closely to the Divine Spirit, this latter wisdom is communicated especially to chiefs, judges, counsellors, and kings. In later sapiential literature a confluence of these two wisdom currents is recognizable.[22]

This ambivalent nature of Judaic wisdom can be understood only in discussing each of its representations independently. The first of these is more commonly the subject of the didactic, moralistic "poetry of wisdom." The natural, rational, totally practical wisdom of experience is constantly praised and recommended throughout the sapiential books by the sages of Israel. It represents an acquired *savoir-faire,* a success formula for a happy life lived in obedience to the Law. There is an unmistakable Hellenic influence in this wisdom, for it is but the expression in scriptural imagery of the prudence of Aristotle and the later *recta ratio agibilium* of scholasticism.[23] At the same time this wisdom is not completely identified with the wisdom of the neighboring cultures. While the latter is a pure "humanism," the wisdom of religion-rooted Israel is rather a "devout humanism," a quality which becomes more evident with the progress of revelation.[24]

[22]In *Job, Ecclesiasticus, Baruch* and *Wisdom,* according to the view of Van Imschoot, "Sagesse et esprit," pp. 23-24. According to Porteous, however, the two thought trends continued in simple juxtaposition: "Along side of what has been called the democratization of wisdom into the prudence which should govern ordinary human life in all its variety, there continued in Israel the conviction that wisdom was required in quite a special way by those who were charged with the duty of government, and that this eventually had important theological consequences (Christ)," in "Royal Wisdom," p. 253. Apparently, Fr. Roland Murphy does not want to speak of Old Testament wisdom as radically two-dimensional. He refers rather to the "many facets to the concept of wisdom." *Seven Books,* p. 143.

[23]Cf. Spicq, "La vertu de prudence," p. 209. See also R. de Vaux, O.P., "Le livre de la sagesse: introduction" in *La Sainte Bible*—Jérusalem (Paris: Les éditions du Cerf, 1956), p. 868.

[24]Cf. R. de Vaux, O.P., "Les livres sapientiaux: introduction" in *La Sainte Bible*—Jérusalem (Paris: Les éditions du Cerf, 1956), p. 597.

A theology of wisdom

With this Israelitic prudence as a background, the second wisdom stands out as something far more mysterious, even while merging imperceptibly with the first. It is a wisdom of divine origin, personifying an attribute of God and, in certain texts, suggesting the divine personality itself.[25] Feminine in personification, she is everywhere, all-powerful, extending her influence to all of creation, cherished by the Master of the universe. Intellectual and moral perfections abound in her.[26] The source of knowledge and happiness and immortality, of all good things, she is desirable above all else, and "the desire of wisdom leads to the (everlasting) kingdom."[27]

In all the wisdom literature, whether the emphasis is placed upon acquired human prudence or upon the more divine and personal wisdom communicated to men by God, there is evident an accent distinctly practical.[28] Even in the more sublime poetry describing Divine Wisdom as personified, wisdom enters the picture, not exclusively but almost invariably, to introduce moral exhortations. Old Testament wisdom seems, therefore, to be essentially prudential. It is true that in several passages there is a hint of speculative values in Judaic wisdom[29]; however, the stress never rests there. Abstracting from the possible Trinitarian intimations, the texts of the Old Testament present a practical wisdom, rational, moral, religious. Because of this, the dependence of St. Thomas upon the sapiential books is considerably reduced, for in his conception, as we shall see

[25]The question whether or not a distinct divine personality (Word or Spirit) can be inferred from certain Old Testament texts is controverted and quite beyond our consideration here.

[26]"Du point de vue intellectuel, l'esprit de sagesse est intelligent, unique et multiple tout ensemble, subtil, agile, pénétrant et aiguisé, sûr, constant et inébranlable, dégagé et libéré de tout, il peut tout, il voit tout; c'est dire sa force de pénétration, son immanence, sa solidité, sa puissance et sa liberté. Du point de vue moral, il est saint, sans souillure, incapable de blesser, généreux, bienfaisant, humain." Duesberg, *Les scribes inspirés,* pp. 491-92. Cf. the profound, descriptive verses in *Wisdom,* chap. 7.

[27]*Wis.* 6:20.

[28]Cf. Botte, "La sagesse," p. 85.

[29]Cf. *Prov.* 8, *Job* 28, *Ecclus.* 24, and *Wis.* 9, according to Baumgartner, *Israëlitische und altorientalische Weisheit,* p. 28.

later, the primacy is always speculative among the various habits of wisdom.   ·

B. WISDOM IN THE NEW TESTAMENT[30]

The transition from the sapiential books to the New Testament is not an abrupt change to an entirely different concept of wisdom. Christianity presents rather a continuation of Judaic wisdom, completing the portrait begun by the wise men of Israel and elevating revealed wisdom to its full perfection. Scattered allusions to wisdom, as it is revealed in Christ, are contained in the Gospels, but it is St. Paul who puts the final touches to revelation's sapiential image.[31] Our study here, therefore, will examine primarily Pauline thought.

In other epistles St. Paul is content to present the treasures of divine wisdom without the pejorative allusions made to human wisdom so evident in the first and second chapters of *I Corinthians*. In this epistle he is forced by the sophistic eloquence of Corinthian intellectuals to set the wisdom of the flesh in sharp contrast to the wisdom of the spirit. The reproaches are not directed against human wisdom as such but to its abuse, a perversion of rhetoric, giving birth to a mere verbal wisdom. To the sophism of Corinth the Christian message appears as stupid and foolish, because even the natural knowledge the Greeks possessed of God had been denied its fruit of adoration.

[30]Cf. the following works: E. Allo, O.P., "Sagesse et Pneuma dans la première épitre aux Corinthiens," *Revue biblique*, 43 (1934) 321-46; J. de Finance, "La ΣΟΦΙΑ chez St. Paul," *Recherches des sciences religieuses*, 25 (1935) 385-417; H. Duesberg, O.S.B., *Les scribes inspirés* (Paris: Desclée de Brouwer, 1939); J. Dupont, O.S.B., *Gnosis. La connaissance religieuse dans les épitres de St. Paul* (Paris: Desclée de Brouwer, 1949); A. Feuillet, P.S.S., "Jésus et la Sagesse Divine après les évangiles synoptiques," *Revue biblique*, 62 (1955) 161-96; F. Prat, S.J., *La théologie de St. Paul*, Vol. I, (Paris: Beauchesne, 1912); C. Spicq, O.P., "Epitres aux Corinthiens, traduites et commentées," *La Sainte Bible*—Pirot-Clamer, Tome XI (Paris: Letouzey et Ané, 1951).

[31]M.-E. Boismard, O.P., commenting on the Gospel according to St. John, suggests that wisdom as personal, subsistent, and eternal is precisely the message of St. John. Cf. notes on *Jn.* 1:1 & 6:35 in *La Sainte Bible*—Jérusalem (Paris: Les éditions du Cerf, 1956), pp. 1397 & 1406. See also the note of H. Duesberg, O.S.B., on *Prov.* 8:22ff., *Ibid.*, p. 810. It seems true, however, that St. Paul presents far more explicitly the New Testament doctrine on wisdom.

11

Human speculation in Greek culture had prostituted itself to its own end; it had sought and loved more the knowledge of the truth than the truth itself.[32] This is why St. Paul is so devastatingly critical.

In opposition to this corrupted rhetoric, St. Paul outlines the wisdom of the spirit, in its essence the marvelous economy of salvation, the mystery of God's plan with Christ at the center uniting all things. "Wisdom, the eminent property of God, is no longer that which is manifested in nature and history, and which the wise of this world should have known; it is a superior wisdom, a mystery which the human intelligence discovers only through divine revelation."[33] At the heart of that mystery is the Cross and Christ crucified, "to the Jews indeed a stumbling-block and to the Gentiles foolishness, but to those who are called, both Jews and Greeks, Christ, the power of God and the *wisdom* of God."[34] The paradox of Christianity is nowhere more apparent as St. Paul, using a finished rhetoric he modestly denies to be his, effectively demonstrates how wondrously wise is the foolishness of accepting Christ.

The wisdom of the New Testament has for its object the whole Christian revelation; but it is more concerned with the mystery of God's will and his plan for all humanity than with his nature and attributes. The witness to this wisdom and its personification is Christ, who now reveals the divine secrets to us through his Spirit.[35] Subjectively, the virtue of faith and the gifts perfecting it bring to men that wisdom[36]; and the degree in which they surrender themselves to the operation of the Spirit, the measure of their taking on "the mind of Christ," will determine their participation in the "wisdom of God." The spiritual

[32]Cf. de Finance, "La ΣΟΦΙΑ," pp. 392-94.
[33]"La sagesse, propriété éminente de Dieu, n'est plus celle qui est manifestée dans la nature et dans l'histoire, et que les sages de ce monde auraient dû connaître (1 Cor. 1:21); c'est une sagesse supérieure et comme un mystère, que l'intelligence humaine ne peut découvrir qu'à l'aide de la révélation divine." Spicq, "Epitres aux Corinthiens," p. 187.
[34]*I Cor.* 1:23-24.
[35]*Ibid.*, 2:6-16. Cf. Dupont, *Gnosis*, pp. 16-17.
[36]Cf. Allo, "Sagesse et Pneuma," p. 345.

man is able to judge all things, because his union with Christ in the Spirit gives to him the very thought of Christ.[37]

Moving beyond the profane wisdom of philosophical speculation and the Old Testament portrait of wisdom as the charming daughter of the Most High, but in direct opposition to the verbal wisdom of the sophists, St. Paul presents the wisdom of Christianity which is totally Christocentric. It is not a grasp of abstract essences and laws, but a penetration into the existential actuality of things, seeing them as they really exist and ranging them in order under the dominating unity of Christ. Whatever may be lost in necessity and comprehension is gained in richness and depth. The Christian universe is viewed in its concrete orientation, wherein salvation is at stake, adding an element of risk and tragedy. All this mocks the traditional serene smile of the Greeks, and for those who see the perfection of the intellect only in the abstract understanding of essences and laws, Christianity must in its depth remain unintelligible.[38]

This dimension of realism found in the New Testament will be echoed in later writers, though certainly not always with its Christian overtones. Yet, for a modern world, reminded by men like Kierkegaard, Nietzsche, Heidegger, Jaspers, and Sartre of the importance of man's concrete, existential situation, wisdom's realism should be impressive. If wisdom is really involved in man's involvement, then its implications deserve our attention. That consideration must wait, however, for our attention here is given to history.

III. WISDOM IN ST. AUGUSTINE[39]

The concept of wisdom in post-revelation Christianity found its greatest admirer in St. Augustine, for whom wisdom was the

---

[37] *I Cor.* 2:15-16. Cf. Spicq, "Epitres aux Corinthiens," p. 190.
[38] Cf. de Finance, "La ΣΟΦΙΑ," pp. 416-17.
[39] Cf. the following works: F. Cayré, A.A., *La contemplation augustinienne* (Paris: Desclée de Brouwer, 1954); *Id.*, "Introduction aux oeuvres de Saint Augustin," *Oeuvres de Saint Augustin* (Paris: Desclée de Brouwer, 1949)

unum necessarium. His writings abound with allusions to his beloved *sapientia,* and although the notion remains always somewhat veiled in the clear-obscure, the absence of precise distinctions does not lessen the richness of the idea. Here, because Augustine's thought had a greater influence on the thirteenth century than that of any other Christian writer, our study of the period of the Fathers must be focused upon the Augustinian concept of wisdom.

A. RELIGIOUS WISDOM

For St. Augustine, true wisdom comes only to him who accepts the folly of the Cross, of which St. Paul speaks so eloquently. In the ascending stages of spiritual life, outlined by a contemporary writer on St. Augustine, wisdom is introduced only when the soul, transformed by faith, begins to seek to understand revealed truths, and reaches its term only in the pure, limpid, certain contemplation of those truths.[40] Without faith man is incapable of understanding truth: "Unless you believe, you will not understand"[41] is a favorite text of St. Augustine. But this must be completed by its counterpart: "Unless you love, you will not understand," which is equally as vital in the Augustinian doctrine. There can be no wisdom, no ultimate understanding, no perfect knowledge of God, that is not at the same time affective: ". . . no good can be perfectly known

pp. 46-99; *Id.* "La notion de sagesse chez Saint Augustin," *L'Année théologique,* 4 (1943) 433-56; T. Deman, O.P., "Composantes de la théologie," *Revue des sciences philosophiques et théologiques,* 28 (1939) 386-434; R. Gagnebet, O.P., *De natura theologiae eiusque methodo secundum Sanctum Thomam,* Vol. I (Rome: Angelicum, 1950); *Id.,* "La nature de la théologie spéculative," *Revue thomiste,* 44 (1938) 1-39, 213-55, 645-74; E. Gilson, *Introduction à l'étude de Saint Augustin* (Paris: Vrin, 1943); J. Maritain, *Distinguer pour unir ou Les degrés du savoir* (Paris: Desclée de Brouwer, 1932); H. I. Marrou, *Saint Augustin et la fin de la culture antique* (Paris: Boccard, 1938 . . . "Retractatio," 1949); E. Portalié, "Augustin," *Dictionnaire de théologie catholique,* Tome I, col. 2268-2472; F. Thonnard, A.A., "Science et sagesse dans la cité de Dieu," *La Ciudad de Dios,* 167 (1954) 511-24.

[40]Gilson, *Introduction,* pp. 159-63.

[41]*Isa.* 7:9.

unless it be perfectly loved."[42] Here we touch the heart of Augustinian wisdom. The faith which introduces man to the wisdom of Christianity must be living, it must be bathed in the light of charity and the gifts of the Holy Spirit.[43] Only in this sense can we understand the principle to which St. Augustine returns again and again: "The wisdom of man is sanctity."[44]

It must be remembered that the central problem for St. Augustine is the nature of happiness and where it is to be found.[45] For him, happiness is nothing else than wisdom and its principal act, "contemplation of the truth, knowledge of God, a knowledge which is without doubt also vision, contact, love, participation, but above all certitude."[46] Ultimately, there is very little which wisdom is not—it embraces all the Christian values, intellectual and moral, in characterizing as it does, the state of perfection, where the soul is anchored in love by interior peace and the habitual joy in God, which is the fruit of charity.[47] In defining Augustinian wisdom, one of its foremost commentators distills the following from its most apparent traits: "A piety profoundly illuminated by faith and animated by hope and charity. However," he adds, "to understand its deepest meaning with all that the saint gives to the word (wisdom) of light, force and love, we prefer to say: Augustinian wisdom is the

---

[42]". . . nullumque bonum perfecte noscitur quod non perfecte amatur." *De Diversis Quaestionibus*, q. 35, no. 2, P.L. 40:24 (cited by Gagnebet, "La nature," p. 37).

[43]Cf. Cayré, *La contemplation augustinienne*, p. 124. See also Thonnard, "Science et sagesse," pp. 515 & 521.

[44]"Hominis sapientia pietas est." *Enchiridion*, c. 2, P.L. 40:231; *De Civitate Dei*, XIV, c. 28, P.L. 41:436; *De Spiritu et Littera*, c. 13, no. 22, P.L. 44:264 (cited by Portalié, "Augustin," col. 2432).

[45]H. I. Marrou, *Saint Augustin*, p. 174.

[46]". . . la sagesse pour lui est toujours restée une contemplation de la vérité, une connaissance de Dieu, connaissance qui est sans doute aussi vision, contact, amour, participation, mais avant tout certitude." *Ibid.*, p. 363. Cf. Gilson, *Introduction*, p. 7. The intellectual life finds all its meaning, its *raison d'être*, in the quest for happiness: "Nulla est homini causa philosophandi, nisi ut sit beatus." *De Civitate Dei*, XIX, c. 1, P.L. 41:623.

[47]Cayré, "Introduction," p. 89.

interior conformity of the soul to God who lives in her by grace and charity."[48]

We are obviously far removed from something purely intellectual, purely speculative. St. Augustine, like St. Paul, was too existentially minded to disregard man's supernatural involvement. If wisdom is so all-important, it must include charity, for without charity there can be no union with God, no happiness, and therefore, no wisdom. At the very heart of Christian life and perfection wisdom cannot be merely speculative; it is essentially affective.

B. WISDOM AND SCIENCE

A problem remains, however; it is the relationship that exists between wisdom and science, a constantly recurring duality in Augustinian thought. If wisdom is everything, what is science? "Wisdom is the science of human and divine things," writes St. Augustine.[49] But he goes on to distinguish the two more clearly: ". . . this definition must be divided so that the science of divine things be named properly *wisdom*, while that of human things be given the name, *science*."[50] As E. Gilson comments:

> On the one hand we have a knowledge of the intellect or superior reason turned toward the Divine Ideas, immersed in the order of contemplation, based upon an act of submission to God and beatifying: *wisdom*. On the other hand, we have a knowledge of the inferior reason, directed toward things of sense, of the order of action, based upon an act of avarice and degrading: *science*.[51]

[48]"Une piété hautement éclairée par la foi et animée par l'espérance et la charité. Cependant, à l'envisager en profondeur, avec tout ce qu'en ce mot le saint groupe de lumière, de force et d'amour, nous préférions dire: La sagesse augustinienne est une haute conformité intérieure de l'âme à Dieu qui vit en elle par la grâce et la charité." Cayré, *La contemplation augustinienne*, p. 266.

[49]"Sapientia est rerum humanarum divinarumque scientia," *De Trinitate*, XIV, c. 1, P.L. 42:1037.

[50]". . . ista definitio dividenda est, ut rerum divinarum scientia proprie sapientia nuncupetur, humanarum autem proprie scientia nomen obtineat." *Ibid.*

[51]"D'une part, nous avons une connaissance de l'intellect ou de la raison supérieure tournée vers les Idées divines, de l'ordre de la con-

Here we meet the radical dualism in the Augustinian concept of wisdom and science. While science is concerned with the created, the temporal, the order of means, wisdom looks to the uncreated, the eternal, the kingdom of ends.

H. I. Marrou in his excellent *Saint Augustin et la fin de la culture antique* presents various significations which each of these words is given throughout the works of St. Augustine.[52] He points out that what is original in St. Augustine's concept of science is precisely its opposition to wisdom in the sense outlined above.[53] Wisdom's contemplation of eternal truths is contrasted with the knowledge of things terrestrial, pragmatically considered in view of man's life on earth. To wisdom is reserved the knowledge of God, which is at the same time love—it is at once philosophical and mystical. For St. Augustine, wisdom not only regards its object from the highest point of view, i.e., God, and arranges hierarchically all things according to their respective value; it also adds to the abstractions of scientific analysis the intuitions of love. Identifying itself with piety, it is "the Christian spirit which takes hold of man as a whole, individual and society, in order to unite him to God and lead him to eternal life. This is without doubt the most Augustinian notion (of wisdom) . . ."[54]

templation, fondée sur un acte de soumission à Dieu et beatifiante: la sagesse. D'autre part, nous avons une connaissance de la raison inférieure, tournée vers les choses sensibles, de l'ordre de l'action, fondée sur un acte d'avarice et dégradante: la science." *Introduction*, pp. 157-58.

[52]For *science*, pp. 559-64; for *wisdom*, pp. 564-69. While Marrou isolates 13 different meanings of *wisdom*, F. Cayré, in "La notion de sagesse," lists 31 significations. However, as Marrou suggests in his "Retractatio," published eleven years after the original work and after the appearance of Cayré's enumeration: "C'est qu'il n'y a pas 13 (his own number of variations on wisdom), 31 ou X sens du mot *sapientia;* il y a un certain nombre de phrases augustiniennes où apparaît ce mot et il n'est pas possible de le considérer comme défini hors des divers contextes où il apparaît enrobé." p. 642, note 18.

[53]*Ibid.*, p. 563.

[54]"(La sagesse) s'identifie ainsi avec l'esprit Chrétien qui saisit tout l'homme, individu et société, pour l'unir à Dieu et le conduire à la vie éternelle. Voilà sans doute la notion la plus augustinienne . . ." Cayré, "Introduction," p. 98.

A theology of wisdom

Throughout this brief exposition of St. Augustine's concept of wisdom, it is clear that the distinction made among the various wisdoms, philosophical, theological, mystical, is not Augustinian but much later in origin. There is ultimately but one wisdom for St. Augustine, infused wisdom, which may use the lesser discursive processes and carry their fruit in its train, but which must remain the unique human realization of Divine Wisdom.[55] Supernaturalized throughout, resounding with affective overtones coloring the fundamental that is charity, this sapiential concept was destined to influence profoundly the Christian intellectual world throughout succeeding centuries. Not before the thirteenth century would it be shaded by any nuance of meaning or altered by any shift of emphasis.

IV. WISDOM IN TRANSITION

The transition from the world of St. Augustine to the world of St. Thomas moved through eight centuries of continued emphasis placed upon the affective dimension in wisdom; after all, *sapientia* finds its etymological roots in *sapor*, and is not charity the end of everything? When the established religion of philosophical Platonism was challenged, however, by the introduction of Aristotle in the west, the somewhat over-simplified identification of speculative and practical elements was placed in question. For Aristotle, no expert in Latin philology, and for whom the Gospel message was still non-existent, wisdom, pure and simple, is only speculative, and to make it something essentially affective would seem to him a perversion of its nature. Quite naturally, therefore, the Christian intellectual arena was alive with controversy. Because for the thirteenth-century mind philosophers were non-Christian by definition,[56]

[55]Cf. Maritain, *Les degrés,* p. 588. See also Marrou, *Saint Augustin* (Retractatio), p. 638.

[56]"Le terme *philosophi* désigne ainsi, à l'encontre de philosophia, les philosophes paiens comme tels." M. D. Chenu, O.P., *La théologie au douzième siècle* (Paris: Vrin, 1957), p. 116, note 2. See also pp. 154 & 376.

while the Churchmen (Christians) were theologians, the question at hand was formed immediately in terms of the nature of theology rather than of metaphysics. "Is theology, obviously a Christian wisdom, speculative or affective (practical)?" became the central question.

In the strict Augustinian tradition the answer was categorically in favor of "affective."[57] From St. Anselm's *fides quaerens intellectum*—faith seeking understanding—a faithful echo of St. Augustine's thought at the beginning of scholasticism, to the writings of St. Bonaventure, St. Albert and Robert Kilwardby, the doctrine on the nature of theology carried a distinctly affective base.[58] It was St. Thomas who, accepting Aristotle's position on the intellectual virtues, brought into focus the speculative values inherent in the notion of wisdom. Together with this re-evaluation of speculative excellence, he introduced the distinctions separating metaphysics formally from theology and these two wisdoms from the gift of the Holy Spirit.[59] But these apparently extreme departures from Augustinian tradition were really not as extreme as a cursory reading of doctrinal and historical commentaries might lead one to believe[60]; this should become evident in the chapters that follow.

Cf. *Id.*, "Les philosophes dans la philosophie chrétienne médiévale," *Revue des sciences philosophiques et théologiques,* 26 (1937) 27-40; E. R. Curtius, "Zur Geschichte des Wortes Philosophie im Mittelalter," *Romanische Forschungen,* 57 (1943) 290-309; also St. Thomas, *Summa Theologiae,* II-II, q. 19, a. 7, c.

[57]The word "strict" is used to preclude any implication that St. Thomas stands in contradiction to St. Augustine on the subject of wisdom's nature. Such a position is at best questionable.

[58]Other names, such as Alexander of Hales, William of Melitona, Odo Rigald, etc., could be included. Cf. M. Grabmann, *Die theologische Erkenntnis- und Einleitungslehre des heiligen Thomas von Aquin*—Thomistische Studien, Band IV (Freiburg in S: Paulusverlag, 1948), pp. 189-237; also Gagnebet, "La nature," pp. 1-39.

[59]It is true that St. Bonaventure's remarks in his Commentary, *In III Sent.*, D. 35, q. 2, suggest these distinctions, but he is speaking specifically of science and not of wisdom, and his notion of theology as *"nihilominus acquisita"* does not coincide with the second member of St. Thomas's three wisdoms.

[60]Cf. Maritain, *Les degrés,* p. 611: ". . . c'est dans la synthèse thomiste-même où St. Augustin vit encore." See also: Deman, "Composantes," pp. 429-30: "St. Thomas y (first question of his *Summa Theologiae*)

A theology of wisdom

V. THE THOUGHT OF ST. THOMAS

ORGANIZATION OF A COMPARATIVE STUDY

In the conception of St. Thomas there is first a purely natural wisdom whose light is that of human reason alone; and although he speaks of lesser (*secundum quid*) realizations of this wisdom, such as prudence and the various arts, its title belongs rightfully (*simpliciter*) to metaphysics. A second wisdom finds its beginning in faith, *fides quaerens intellectum*, whose light, no longer merely that of reason, is rather reason illumined by faith.[61] Finally, above these two acquired wisdoms, for both are rational structures, there is the wisdom, gift of the Holy Spirit, whose light is discovered in the affective connaturality realized by charity. This three-fold conception, embracing natural reason, Christian reason and the Holy Spirit as principles of three wisdoms, as they are principles of man's acts[62], is peculiarly Thomistic; for this reason, its study must concern primarily the writings of St. Thomas.

Within the Thomistic wisdom triad there is another element, suggested above, which demands attention in any serious attempt to construct a theology of wisdom. It is precisely the dimension of affectivity involved in wisdom, abstracting from the latter's particular realizations. Obvious enough in the gift of wisdom, it is not quite so evident in metaphysics and theology, where it remains a problem whose solution is not unimportant. Does

établit expressément que la théologie est sagesse: il rejoint alors, quoique selon une détermination inspirée d'Aristote, l'idée augustinienne que ce mot recouvre et qui est d'ailleurs un bien de la philosophie; St. Thomas déclare en toutes lettres cette rencontre et on peut l'en croire."; E. Gilson, *History of Christian Philosophy in the Middle Ages* (London: Sheed & Ward, 1955), pp. 81, 364.

[61]Faith alone, perhaps, might be considered a wisdom, for it is a knowledge of the highest cause. However, faith is not, strictly speaking, causal knowledge; and because it is open to the structural development of reason and to the illuminating affectivity of charity, it seems more accurate to speak of faith as properly an inchoative wisdom, not yet realized. Cf. *infra*, pp. 62-63.

[62]Cf. F. Marin-Sola, O.P., *L'évolution homogène du Dogme catholique* (Fribourg: Imprimerie de St. Paul, 1924) I, 389-90.

affectivity, for example, have any place at all in metaphysics? And whether or not it belongs in metaphysics, can it enter the world of theology without being considered an intruder? There are, incidentally, some writers who see in St. Thomas's doctrine on wisdom a return to Plato's position, associating far more closely, if not identifying, the speculative with the practical or affective.[63] But any judgment regarding this must await the light of the texts to be examined later.

The organization of the present study, therefore, will be centered around the three wisdoms: metaphysics, theology, and the gift of wisdom, with a chapter devoted to each. The plan within the chapters will follow basically the scientific questions inherited from Aristotle: *an sit—quid sit—qualis sit.*[64] However, the problems peculiar to the *an sit* of each wisdom will be treated only cursorily, because what is more important and what explains ultimately the *an sit* is the understanding of the nature of each wisdom or its *quid sit.* In considering the *qualis sit* or the properties of the three wisdoms it seems necessary to distinguish the principal or primary act of wisdom from those acts which either serve or follow upon that act. Therefore, in order to make this supremacy more apparent, the principal or primary act will be treated in connection with the respective *quid sit* of each wisdom, while the other acts—more properly called functions—will be reserved to the consideration of *qualis sit.* Throughout the study the dimension of affectivity proper to each wisdom will be considered as well as the progressive completion of an inferior by a superior wisdom.

With this brief survey as a point of departure we begin here under the guidance of St. Thomas the study *toward a theology of wisdom.*

---

[63]Cf. J. Lenz, "Thomistische Philosophie als Lebensweisheit," *Pastor Bonus,* 49 (1939-40) 323-47; J. Hirschberger, "Quod sit officium sapientis," *Philosophisches Jahrbuch,* 53 (1940) 30-44.

[64]The question, *qualis sit,* here embraces both dimensions of the investigation of properties: *quia* (the fact that something is of such a kind) and *propter quid* (precisely why it is of such a kind).

II

THE WISDOM OF
METAPHYSICS

In the vast field of purely human or natural knowledge, what part can be given the name, *wisdom?* We speak of wise doctors, wise architects, wise men in general. They are considered wise who have a moral or prudential grasp of what should or should not be done or, perhaps, just a practical sense guided by purely pragmatic considerations. But is this wisdom human wisdom in the fullest sense? The ordering of means to ends, no matter what particular activity is involved, seems to represent nothing more than a share in wisdom's traditionally recognized right to order; and in each of the cases mentioned above the ordering implied is only practical. Does this mean that wisdom can be only practical? If so, which of these essentially practical forms of knowledge will be wisdom? Will it be medicine or architecture, or will it be the highly developed moral sense or possibly the general "know-how" of the man we call practical? Or might it be true that human wisdom cannot exclude the realm of speculative values, and in its highest form it is not practical but speculative?

We have seen earlier that for Aristotle wisdom is only speculative, because for him the essential criterion of wisdom is knowledge of highest causes.[1] This particular conception

---

[1] Cf. *supra,* pp. 3-7.

22

which demands that the wise man have a knowledge of God, the unique highest cause, became the basis for the thought of St. Thomas on wisdom.[2] In the natural order, where the intellectual light is human reason, there is for St. Thomas, as for Aristotle, but one branch of knowledge which places man in contact with God as highest cause. It is what Aristotle calls first philosophy or theology (divine science)—which we name metaphysics.

I. THE APPROACH TO METAPHYSICS THROUGH THE PHILOSOPHY OF NATURE

A. STATEMENT OF THE PROBLEM

The question of the existence of metaphysics, the *an sit* of what is truly human wisdom according to Aristotle and St. Thomas, will not involve here precisely the problem of affirming or denying that there is a metaphysics. The existence of metaphysics is readily admitted by most philosophers and, certainly, by anyone speaking in a context of Christian philosophy. What remains problematic and in controversy today is the proper approach to metaphysics. How does the mind arrive at its study? Such a question concerns the isolation of a subject proper to metaphysics, for before constructing a science, a subject proper to that science must be determined.

The subject of metaphysics is being, formally qualified as being *qua* being (*ens inquantum ens*), a phrase which is meant to embrace immaterial as well as material reality. The problem at hand, therefore, is reduced to this: Can the subject of metaphysics, involving as it does both immaterial and material being, be isolated without demonstrating the existence of something immaterial? In other words, is an intuition of being, which is not reinforced or sustained by certified knowledge of some

[2]This will be made evident in the texts cited throughout the following pages. Here, to choose one text among many others, cf. *Cont. Gent.* IV, 12: "Sapientia in homine dicitur habitus quidam quo mens nostra perficitur in cognitione altissimorum: et huiusmodi sunt divina."

immaterial existence, enough to give to metaphysics a subject of study proper to itself?

B. SOLUTION TO THE PROBLEM

According to Aristotle and St. Thomas, the answer seems to be in the negative. Unless the existence of immaterial being is demonstrated, then reality is apparently exhausted by material being and belongs properly to the study of physics or philosophy of nature. The simple intuition of being might introduce the immaterial world hypothetically but hardly scientifically. St. Thomas writes:

> If there is no other substance besides those which exist according to nature, the proper concern of physics, then physics will be the supreme science. But if there exists some immobile substance, this will be prior to natural substance; and consequently the philosophy considering such a substance will be first philosophy.[3]

And again: "If, however, there is besides natural substances another nature or substance which is separable and immobile, this necessitates another science, one superior to physics."[4]

On the supposition that there exists nothing beyond the material world of mobile being, the primacy among the sciences would be attributed to the philosophy of nature. There would be no metaphysics, because its subject would be no different from that of physics.[5] It is only after we become aware that

---

[3]"Si non est aliqua alia substantia praeter eas quae consistunt secundum naturam, de quibus est physica, physica erit prima scientia. Sed si est aliqua substantia immobilis, ista erit prior substantia naturali; et per consequens philosophia considerans huiusmodi substantiam erit philosophia prima." *In VI Meta.*, lect. 1, no. 1170. Cf. Aristotle, *Metaphysics*, Bk. VI, c. 1 (1026 a 28-30).

[4]"Si autem est alia natura et substantia praeter substantias naturales, quae sit separabilis et immobilis, necesse est alteram scientiam ipsius esse, quae sit prior naturali." *In XI Meta.*, lect. 7, no. 2267. Cf. also *In III Meta.*, lect. 6, no. 398.

[5]Cf. W. H. Kane, O.P., "Abstraction and the Distinction of the Sciences," *The Thomist*, 17 (1954) 43-68. "The important initial question is whether all beings are sensory and material or whether there are also immaterial beings. If all beings are material, then physics or natural science is First Philosophy and there is no need for metaphysics. . . . In physics we prove that there is an Unmoved Mover and that the soul

there exist material and immaterial beings that the subject of metaphysics can be established. Otherwise, the problems we know as metaphysical should be treated by the philosopher of nature, as was the case among the philosophers before Aristotle:

> Certain philosophers of nature applied themselves to these problems (the general problems of metaphysics) and not without reason. For the ancients were not aware that there exists some substance other than the material, mobile substance of which physics treats. And therefore it was believed that they alone were competent to treat the whole of nature and consequently being and the first principles whose consideration must follow upon the consideration of being. This however is false . . . since in the eighth book of the *Physics* it is demonstrated that there exists some immobile being.[6]

This usurping of the metaphysicians' rights was conditioned by the ignorance of immaterial being, whose existence is the final consideration of the philosophy of nature.[7] The determination of what it means to be separable from matter is left to metaphysics or first philosophy[8], which treats of "things speculative which do not depend upon matter for their existence because, whether they be such that never exist in matter, as God or an angel, or whether they be found sometimes in matter and sometimes not, as is the case of substance, quality, potency,

---

is a principle of immaterial operations, and so we know that there are beings which are not material beings. . . . If we grant the existence of beings both material and immaterial, then there is a valid foundation for the objective precision by which a sensory being is conceived either as naturally mobile, or an extended unity or simply as a being." *Ibid.*, pp. 61-63. Cf. also the following articles by the same author: "Introduction to Metaphysics," *The Thomist*, 20 (1957) 121-42; "The Nature and Extent of the Philosophy of Nature," *Ibid.*, 7 (1944) 204-32; and "The Subject of Metaphysics," *Ibid.*, 18 (1955) 503-21.

6"Quidam tamen naturalium de his (the general problems of metaphysics) se intromiserunt; et hoc non sine ratione. Antiqui enim non opinabantur aliquam substantiam esse praeter substantiam corpoream mobilem, de qua physicus tractat. Et ideo creditum est quod soli determinent de tota natura, et per consequens de ente, et ita etiam de primis principiis quae sunt simul consideranda cum ente. Hoc autem falsum est . . . cum probatum est in octavo *Physicorum* esse aliquod ens immobile." St. Thomas, *In IV Meta.*, lect. 5, no. 593.

7Cf. *In II Phys.*, lect. 4, no. 175.

8*Ibid.*

A *theology of wisdom*

act, they can exist without matter . . ."[9] The phrase here *because they can exist without matter* is echoed in other passages concerning the subject of metaphysics. For example:

> Substance, however, which is the intelligible matter of quantity *can exist without quantity*.[10] . . . something which exists separated from matter and motion is possible . . . in another way: in this sense that it is not of its very nature to exist in matter and motion but that it *can exist without matter and motion*.[11] There are certain things which can be abstracted even from common intelligible matter, as being, one, potency and act, etc., which *can also exist without any matter* as is evident in immaterial substances.[12]

How can this capacity for existence outside matter be known, except by demonstrating the fact that there are existent immaterial beings? Any other supposition seems to suggest that metaphysics must begin with St. Thomas's fourth proof for God's existence, but without recourse to efficient causality upon which that proof rests. To hold that an intuition of being, with only sensible, material being as its point of departure, is sufficient to establish the notion, *ens commune*, is unsupportable. Such a position would demand an immediate ascent to an immaterial world; but deprived of the certain basis of causality, this must evaporate into mere hypothesis. It seems far more reasonable to recognize the dependence of metaphysics upon the philosophy of nature. In the study of motion the philosopher reaches ultimately an immaterial cause of that motion, while at the same time terminating his investigation of cognitive

[9]Speculabilia quae non dependunt a materia secundum esse, quia sine materia esse possunt, sive nunquam sint in materia, sicut Deus et angelus, sive in quibusdam sint in materia et in quibusdam non, ut substantia, qualitas, potentia, actus . . ." *In Boet. De Trin.*, q. 5, a. 1, c.

[10]"Substantia autem quae est materia intelligibilis quantitatis, *potest esse sine quantitate*." *Ibid.*, a. 3, c.

[11]". . . potest esse aliquid a materia et motu separatum secundum esse . . . alio modo sic quod non sit de ratione eius quod sit in materia et motu sed *possit esse sine materia et motu*." *Ibid.*, a. 4, c.

[12]"Quaedam vero sunt quae possunt abstrahi etiam a materia intelligibili communi, sicut ens, unum, potentia et actus, et alia huiusmodi, quae etiam *esse possunt absque omni materia*, ut patet in substantiis immaterialibus." *Summa* I, q. 85, a. 1, ad 2.

activity in the realization of the soul's independence of matter. Here we arrive at the threshold of metaphysics: Being is not convertible with mobile being; it transcends the merely sensible and material to embrace also a world of immateriality.[13]

This doctrine is implicit in St. Thomas's insistence that metaphysics be taught after the philosophy of nature, as well as in the normal movement of the human mind from the sensible to the intelligible. He writes:

> . . . which by another name is called metaphysics, that is, beyond physics, because we who reach the supra-sensible only through the sensible must learn it after physics.[14] Although divine science is the first among all the sciences, the other sciences are naturally prior for us . . . The order of this science is that it be learned after the natural sciences.[15] Sense knowledge . . . precedes intellectual knowledge in us . . . This science which is called wisdom, although it be first in dignity, is last in the order of learning.[16]

All this is meant to show that the human intellect must grope its way through the opaque world of matter before taking its first faltering steps in quest of human wisdom. The ascent to the summit of immateriality and intelligibility made by reason demands that the summit exist and can be seen in reason's native light. One does not climb a mountain unless there is a mountain to be climbed. And the discovery of the mountain is precisely the service rendered by the philosophy of nature to metaphysics.

---

[13]". . . le jugement négatif qui fonde l'immatérialité de l'objet de la métaphysique tire sa valeur objective de la démonstration de l'existence des êtres immatériels par où s'achève la philosophie de la nature: premier moteur immobile au 8e livre de la *Physique,* âme humaine avec l'intellect agent et l'intellect possible au *Traité de l'âme,*" L. B. Geiger, O.P., "Abstraction et séparation d'après St. Thomas." *Revue des sciences philosophiques et théologiques,* 31 (1947), p. 25.

[14]". . . quae alio nomine dicitur metaphysica, idest trans physicam, quia post physicam discenda occurrit nobis, quibus ex sensibilibus oportet in insensibilia devenire." *In Boet. De Trin.,* q. 5, a. 1, c.

[15]"Quamvis scientia divina sit prima omnium scientiarum, naturaliter, tamen quoad nos aliae scientiae sunt priores . . . ordo huius scientiae est ut addiscatur post scientias naturales." *Ibid.,* a. 1, 9m.

[16]"Cognitio sensus . . . in nobis praecedit cognitionem intellectivam . . . ista scientia, quae sapientia dicitur, quamvis sit prima in dignitate est tamen ultima in addiscendo." *In I Meta.,* lect. 2, no. 46. Cf. also *In VI Eth.,* lect. 7, no. 1211.

II. THE NATURE OF METAPHYSICAL WISDOM AND ITS PRIMARY ACT

After determining the possibility of metaphysics—*ens commune* is a subject distinct from *ens mobile*—what will be the nature of this more universal discipline? Actually, such a reflective question must presuppose an already developed body of knowledge. We assume therefore such a body of knowledge embracing as it must being, together with the principles, properties and causes of being. This is the discipline called metaphysics. But what precisely is its nature and what can be termed its primary act?

The central problem here revolves around the determination of metaphysics as science and as wisdom. And the relationship between these two notions in their applicability to metaphysics is open to different interpretations. At one extreme is the position denying metaphysics the perfection of science, while exalting it as wisdom.[17] At the other extreme is the view that all the perfection of metaphysics as wisdom belongs to it precisely to the extent that it is science and nothing more.[18] But the ever-present necessity of avoiding extremes is not confined to the moral order alone, for *In medio stat virtus* is not exclusively a moral maxim[19]; and this seems to be a case in point. As the paragraphs that follow should bring out, there is a third position, according to which wisdom is at the same time science, yet enjoys prerogatives proper to itself beyond its scientific character. The thematic order of the present section, therefore, will com-

[17]Cf. T. Heath, O.P., *Aristotelian Influence in Thomistic Wisdom: A Comparative Study* (Washington: Catholic University Press, 1956), pp. 7, 8, & passim. Father Heath's work represents an important contribution to the understanding of Aristotelian metaphysics and is especially illuminating in its evaluation of St. Thomas's *Commentary on the Metaphysics*. However, the analysis of the relationship between science and wisdom seems somewhat questionable.

[18]Cf. R. Garrigou-Lagrange, O.P., *De Deo Uno* (Paris: Desclée de Brouwer, 1938), pp. 61-62. The impression given here is that wisdom is nothing more than the most perfect science.

[19]"Inter affirmationes ergo et negationes oppositas accipitur medium virtutum intellectualium speculativarum, quod est verum." *De Virt. In Comm.*, q. un., a. 13, c.

prise first the science-wisdom problem, to be followed by an analysis of metaphysics' principal or primary act.[20]

1. The Virtues of the Speculative Intellect

Among the virtues of the speculative intellect enumerated by Aristotle and echoed by St. Thomas, one is intuitive, *understanding*, the simple grasp of first principles; the other two are discursive, *science*, causal knowledge within a specified genus, and *wisdom*, knowledge through highest causes.[21] Though both science and wisdom are discursive, science demonstrates through inferior causes, while wisdom considers first causes.[22] In virtue of this contact with highest causes, wisdom gains the ascendancy

[20]An observation on method may be helpful here in order to avoid possible confusion later. Any presentation of wisdom according to St. Thomas must begin with his sympathetic exposition of Aristotle for whom there is but one wisdom, that of first philosophy or metaphysics (Cf. Sect. I,B in chap. 1). But a choice must be made. One may either isolate first a common notion of wisdom and then show it to be independently realized in each of the wisdoms distinguished by St. Thomas, or he might combine the analysis of wisdom in general with that of metaphysical wisdom, and then study wisdom's general characteristics as they are realized in theology and the gift of wisdom. The latter method has been our choice, not because it is necessarily more intelligible but because it corresponds more truly to the *via inventionis* exemplified in St. Thomas's own presentation. Here the Aristotelian influence could hardly be more evident.

[21]Cf. Aristotle, *Nicomachean Ethics*, Bk. VI, chaps. 3, 6 & 7 (1139 b 14-1141 b 23); St. Thomas, *Summa* I-II, q. 57, a. 2, c.: "Verum autem est dupliciter considerabile: uno modo, sicut per se notum; alio modo, sicut per aliud notum. Quod autem est per se notum se habet ut principium; et percipitur statim ab intellectu. Et ideo habitus perficiens intellectum ad huiusmodi veri considerationem, vocatur *intellectus* qui est habitus principiorum. Verum autem quod est per aliud notum, non statim percipitur ab intellectu sed per inquisitionem rationis: et se habet in ratione termini. Quod quidem potest esse dupliciter: uno modo, ut sit ultimum in aliquo genere *(scientia)*; alio modo, ut sit ultimum respectu totius cognitionis humanae . . . *sapientia* quae considerat altissimas causas."

[22]"Sapientia et scientia sunt circa partem animae speculativam . . . Differunt autem quia intellectus est habitus principiorum primorum demonstrationis. Scientia vero est conclusionis ex causis inferioribus. Sapientia vero considerat causas primas." *In I Meta.*, lect. 1, no. 34; "Sapientia, scientia et intellectus important rectitudinem cognitionis circa necessaria: scientia quidem circa conclusiones, intellectus autem circa principia, sapientia autem circa causas altissimas quae sunt causae divinae." *In I Post. Anal.*, lect. 44.

over the other two speculative virtues. Understanding is but the habit of simple intuitive assent given to self-evident principles; science is concerned with principles only insofar as they are related to its conclusions; but wisdom not only considers conclusions in the light of principles, it judges the principles themselves, evaluating and defending their content.[23] For this reason, wisdom is said to contain, to be, both understanding and science: "Wisdom is understanding as it judges truth regarding principles; it is science insofar as it knows what is concluded from the principles."[24]

This absorption of understanding and science into wisdom, however, must be understood with certain qualifications. St. Thomas compares wisdom to a potential whole[25] containing understanding and science as potential parts:

> Thus if one considers properly, these three virtues are not distinguished from one another in the same way but in a certain order, as is the case in potential wholes one of whose parts is more perfect than another. For example, the rational soul is more perfect than the sensitive and the sensitive more perfect than the vegetative. In this way science depends upon understanding as upon a superior, and together they depend upon wisdom as supreme, containing within itself both understanding and science as it judges the conclusions of the sciences as well as their principles.[26]

---

[23]"Sapientia non solum utitur principiis indemonstrabilibus, quorum est intellectus, concludendo ex eis, sicut aliae scientiae; sed etiam iudicando de eis, et disputando contra negantes. Unde sequitur quod sapientia sit maior virtus quam intellectus." *Summa* I-II, q. 66, a. 5, ad 4.

[24]"Sapientia inquantum dicit verum circa principia est intellectus: inquantum autem scit ea quae ex principiis concluduntur est scientia." *In VI Eth.*, lect. 5, no. 1188. Cf. also *In I Sent.*, Prol., q. 1, q1a. 1, sol.

[25]"Totum vero potentiale adest singulis partibus secundum totam suam essentiam sed non secundum virtutem." *Summa* I, q. 77, a. 1, ad 1. Cf. the following texts: *De Spir. Creat.*, a. 11, 2m; *In I Sent.*, D. 8, q. 4, a. 2, 1m; *In II Sent.*, D. 9, q. 1, a. 3, 1m; *In IV Sent.*, D. 16, q. 1, a. 1, sol. 3; *Quodl.* X, q. 3, a. 5; *Summa* I, q. 76, a. 8, c. (cited by F. Muniz, O.P., "De diversis muneribus sacrae theologiae secundum doctrinam S. Thomae," *Angelicum* 24 [1947], p. 93, note 1).

[26]"Unde si quis recte considerat, istae tres virtutes non ex aequo distinguuntur ab invicem, sed ordine quodam, sicut accidit in totis potentialibus, quorum una pars est perfectior altera, sicut anima rationalis est

Wisdom thus contains *eminently* the two lesser speculative habits of science and understanding. In the words of one of St. Thomas's commentators: ". . . in wisdom both habits (understanding and science) are contained eminently and formally in one as in something of a superior order."[27] When an inferior power is contained by a superior, the inferior should not be less perfectly but rather more perfectly realized in that superior, as in the rational soul's inclusion of vegetative and sensitive powers. Therefore, wisdom should not be less perfectly but more perfectly science. For the moment, though, let us examine more closely the problem peculiar to the science-wisdom duality, which here concerns metaphysics as both science and wisdom.[28]

2. *Metaphysics: a Wisdom*

As indicated earlier, in speaking of metaphysics and assigning it a place among the intellectual virtues three positions are possible: 1) Metaphysics is not science but wisdom[29]; 2) it is both science and wisdom, but as wisdom there is nothing essential added to its perfection as science—it is merely the highest among the sciences; 3) it is properly wisdom, as well as science, but its sapiential character represents something more than the perfection of science.

perfectior quam sensibilis, et sensibilis quam vegetabilis. Hoc enim modo, scientia dependet ab intellectu sicut a principaliori. Et utrumque dependet a sapientia sicut a principalissimo, quae sub se continet et intellectum et scientiam, ut de conclusionibus scientiarum diiudicans, et de principiis earundem." *Summa* I-II, q. 57, a. 2, ad 2.

[27]". . . in sapientia ambo habitus (intellectus et scientia) in uno eminenter et formaliter tanquam in aliquo superioris ordinis continentur." C. Koellin, *In I-II*, 57, 2, 2m. The text continues: "Scientia autem non includit identice intellectum sed ab eo dependet . . . Sapientia continet sub se scientiam et intellectum non formaliter in propriis naturis quia sic esset habitus compositus sed modo dicto." Cf. also John of St. Thomas, *Curs. Theol.*, In I-II, D. XVI, a. 3, no. 9 (Vives, VI, 466).

[28]This particular problem becomes more important in discussing the nature of theology, where the critique of what is called "conclusion-theology" adds an element of controversy. Cf. *infra*, pp. 69-81.

[29]What is meant here is not the categorical denial of metaphysics as science in favor of wisdom but rather the attempt to exalt metaphysics as wisdom by derogating its perfection as science.

A theology of wisdom

For Aristotle and St. Thomas, the essence of science is certain knowledge through causes gained by means of demonstration.[30] Because there are true demonstrations in metaphysics—the properties of being, God's existence, the divine attributes are all reached through demonstration[31]—metaphysics justifies itself as science, a title attributed to it by St. Thomas throughout his commentary on Aristotle's *Metaphysics*.[32] In the light of this, the first position outlined above seems untenable.

But can it be said that metaphysics is something more than science? Those holding the second position would answer this question affirmatively, yet for them that "something more" would have only nominal significance. As science metaphysics reaches to highest causes and enjoys an exalted perfection; it is therefore given a special name, *wisdom*. This new name, however, is applied simply to the most perfect of sciences.[33] It does not mean that wisdom contains anything that is not already in science. Science is the genus and wisdom its most perfect species. So

[30]Cf. Aristotle, *Posterior Analytics*, Bk. I, c. 2 (71 b 8-19); St. Thomas, *In I Post. Anal.*, lect. 4. On the Aristotelian-Thomistic conception of science and demonstration see M. Glutz, C.P., *The Manner of Demonstrating in Natural Philosophy* (St. Meinrad: Abbey Press, 1956), c. 1, pp. 1-39: "The Aristotelian-Thomistic Concept of Demonstration"; also P. Wyser, O.P., *Theologie als Wissenschaft* (Salzburg: Pustet, 1938), Zweiter Teil, pp. 63-83: "Wesen und Wert des Demonstrativen Erkennens."

[31]The lack of a real distinction between being and its properties or between the divine nature and the divine attributes might seem to vitiate the demonstrative character of metaphysical argumentation. However, the following text of John of St. Thomas meets this difficulty successfully: "De demonstrationibus propter quid, respondetur non requiri quod semper procedant ex causa quae formaliter sit causa et physica, sed sufficit quod virtualiter vel metaphysice, ita quod unum se habeat ut ratio alterius, etsi non sit causans alterum, sicut immutabilitas est ratio aeternitatis et perfectio bonitatis, etc. Quod vero dicitur de prima passione respectu essentiae, respondetur illam quidem causari et dimanare ab essentia sed quia essentia est subiectum, de quo debet demonstrari, non potest demonstrari de ipsa essentia nisi per ipsammet essentiam. Unde in re caret medio, per quod demonstratur, quia est idem cum subiecto; accipitur tamen a nobis definitio essentiae quasi medium demonstrationis non rei, sed ratione distinctum." *Curs. Phil.*, Log., II, Q. XXV, a. 1 (Reiser, I, 775-76).

[32]Cf. also *In Boet. De Trin.*, qq. 5 & 6, passim.

[33]"In his autem in quibus aliquid est perfectissimum nomen commune generis appropriatur his quae deficiunt a perfectissimo, ipsi autem perfectissimo adaptatur aliud speciale nomen." *Summa* II-II, q. 9, a. 2, c. See also *In III Sent.*, D. 35, q. 2, a. 3, sol. 1.

runs the argument. Such a position would be valid if wisdom involved nothing that exceeded the formal character of science: ". . . the *ratio* of science consists in this that from things known one attains the knowledge of things unknown."[34] If wisdom implied merely the movement from principles to conclusions and the return to principles in resolution, it would be nothing more than science; but wisdom includes more than the demonstrative discursus, the *exitus-reditus* of scientific reasoning, for in virtue of its contact with highest causes, it is competent to explain, evaluate, judge, and defend the principles themselves:

> Wisdom is a certain science because it includes that which is common to all sciences, namely, the demonstration of conclusions from principles; but because it possesses *something proper to itself* above the other sciences—insofar as it judges all things and this not only with respect to first principles—it has therefore the character of a more perfect virtue than science.[35]

This is why science cannot be considered a genus in which wisdom is merely the most perfect species.[36] Wisdom embraces

---

[34]". . . scientiae ratio consistat in hoc quod ex aliquibus notis alia ignotiora cognoscantur." *In Boet. De Trin.*, q. 2, a. 2, c. Cf. also *In I Sent.*, Prol., q. 1, sols. 1 & 2; *Summa* I, q. 1, a. 2, c.

[35]"Sapientia est quaedam scientia inquantum habet id quod est commune omnibus scientiis, ut scilicet ex principiis conclusiones demonstret, sed quia habet *aliquid proprium* super alias scientias, inquantum scilicet de omnibus judicat, et non solum quantum ad prima principia: ideo habet rationem perfectioris virtutis quam scientia." *Summa* I-II, q. 57, a. 2, ad 1. "Sapientia non dividitur contra scientiam sicut oppositum contra oppositum; sed quia se habet ex additione ad scientiam. Est enim sapientia, ut dicit Philosophus in VI *Ethicorum,* caput omnium scientiarum, regulans omnes alias, inquantum de altissimis principiis est." *In Boet. De Trin.*, q. 2, a. 2, 1m. See also *In XI Meta.*, lect. 1, no. 2151; *In III Sent.*, D. 35, q. 2, a. 1, q1a. 1, 1m; a. 3, sol. 1.

[36]". . . quia de ratione generis est dicere totum quod est in specie ideo scientia non est proprie genus sapientiae sed magis se habet sicut pars potentialis ad sapientiam, quia includitur et cum hoc sibi aliquid additur per sapientiam . . . Dico enim quod sapientia aliquid dicit quod non includit scientia, nec de significato materiali. Dico enim quod iudicare de principiis est omnino extra rationem scientiae. Et volo bene quod si de ratione sapientiae esset tantum procedere ex principiis primis et altissima causa quod tunc scientia esset genus sapientiae . . . sed nunc habet hoc sapientia et cum hoc judicium alterius rationis, ideo scientia non est genus sed dicit partem inclusam in ratione sapientiae. . . . Et scientia praedicatur formaliter de sapientia; non tamen dicit totam rationem eius sed partem." C. Koellin, *In I-II*, q. 57, a. 2, ad 1. Cf. also the text cited below, note 37.

more than science, and, therefore, demands to be distinguished from science. Unless this were true, there would be no reason to enumerate three speculative intellectual virtues; understanding and science would suffice.[37] However, wisdom connotes "a certain excellence above the common perfection"[38] and so justifies its independence as supreme among the intellectual virtues.

From what has been said above, metaphysics is properly wisdom, but it is also science, for it includes the demonstrative function proper to science.[39] Contrary to the first position, therefore, metaphysics need not be derogated as science in order to be exalted as wisdom—it is both science and wisdom. And because the science in wisdom resolves its conclusions to principles more profoundly understood through wisdom's penetrating judgment, metaphysics should be more profoundly science than the lower disciplines. Against the second position, it is evident that although metaphysics is indeed science, it is more; its nature as wisdom adds to it something over and above its perfection as science, for science is concerned with principles

[37]John of St. Thomas remarks: ". . . in sapientia considerantur duo. Primum est, ex principiis deducere conclusiones et demonstrative procedere: secundum est, universalitas ejus qua se extendit ad judicandum de omnibus, etiam de ipsis principiis, quatenus ea defendit, et explicat, quatenus talia principia ad altissimas causas reducibilia sunt, atque ab eis dependet . . . Si consideretur sapientia primo modo, sic est species quaedam scientiae generaliter sumptae, et convenit illi definitio scientiae posita a Philosopho, cum sapientia sit habitus demonstrativus ex principiis probans conclusiones. Caeterum secundo modo excedit vim et rationem scientiae, non solum quia perfectissima species illius est, sed propter influentiam quam habet in reliquas scientias, et in earum principia judicando, et ordinando de omnibus, atque reducendo ad altissimas causas. Unde fuit necesse numerare hunc habitum inter caeteros et condistinguere a scientia et aliis, quia licet sapientia quaedam scientia sit et habitus demonstrativus, tamen in ratione virtutis intellectualis perficientis intellectum in ratione veri specialem habet eminentiam et excellentiam, quatenus habet ordinare et judicare de omnibus, et de ipsis principiis defendendo et explicando ea, et sic est quasi regula et mensura perficiens reliquas scientias." Curs. Theol., In I-II, Disp. XVI, a. 3, nos. 4 & 5 (Vives, VI, 461-62). This seems to prove incorrect the view making science a genus expressed by J. Peghaire in Intellectus et ratio selon St. Thomas (Paris: Vrin, 1936), p. 157.

[38]". . . aliquam excellentiam super rationem communis" In III Sent., D. 35, q. 2, a. 3, sol. 1.

[39]". . . ad sapientem pertinet quod habeat demonstrationem de aliquibus rebus, idest de primis causis entium." In VI Eth., lect. 5, no. 1177. Cf. also In XI Meta., lect. 1, no. 2155.

only insofar as they are related to its conclusions, not in themselves. Wisdom judges principles themselves. It is true that metaphysics as science may be prior in the order of generation, since the demonstrative function must be exercised to attain highest causes, but in the order of perfection metaphysics as wisdom is prior. It is this wisdom that shall be our study here.

3. *The Sapiential Structure of Metaphysics*

In the Aristotelian-Thomistic picture the wisdom of metaphysics has for its subject being as being, *ens inquantum ens.* This statement may perhaps be questioned by some modern Thomists, who contend that God is the proper subject of metaphysics.[40] Such a contention, however, seems at best founded upon a confusion of the terms "subject" and "object" in scientific study, for the texts of St. Thomas throughout his commentary on the *Metaphysics*[41] are apodictic on this point, and but reaffirm his position in the commentary on Boethius's *De Trinitate.*[42] For

[40]Cf., for example, E. Gilson, *Le thomisme* (Paris: Vrin, 1945), p. 28, and also J. Anderson, *An Introduction to the Metaphysics of St. Thomas Aquinas* (Chicago: Henry Regnery Co., 1953), pp. vii & viii. M. Gilson uses such terms as *object* and *end* but without having clarified his position by distinguishing the *subject* of metaphysics from its *object*. As a result, the reader is left with the impression that in M. Gilson's opinion St. Thomas makes God the *subject* of metaphysics. A similar distinction would have strengthened Mr. Anderson's remark that metaphysics is primarily and principally about God—that is, if he refers to God not as the *subject* of metaphysics but as its supreme *object*.

[41]"Ista scientia . . . considerat . . . ut subiectum solum ens commune . . . Subiectum huius scientiae sit ens commune." *In XII Libros Meta.,* Proem., in fine; ". . . est quaedam scientia quae speculatur ens secundum quod est ens sicut subiectum." *In IV Meta.,* lect. 1, no. 529; "Omnes philosophi elementa quaerentes secundum quod sunt entia quaerebant huiusmodi principia, scilicet prima et altissima; ergo in hac scientia nos quaerimus principia entis inquantum est ens; ergo ens est subiectum huius scientiae, quia quaelibet scientia est quaerens causas proprias sui subiecti." *Ibid.,* no. 533; "De quolibet ente inquantum est ens proprium est metaphysici considerare." *In VI Meta.,* lect. 1, no. 1147.

[42]*In Boet. De Trin.,* q. 5, a. 4, c: "Res divinae non tractantur a philosophis nisi prout sunt rerum omnium principia et ideo pertractantur in illa doctrina (metaphysica) in qua ponuntur ea quae sunt communia omnibus entibus, quae habet subiectum ens inquantum est ens . . . Sic ergo theologia, sive scientia divina, est duplex. Una in qua considerantur res divinae, *non tanquam subiectum scientiae,* sed tanquam principia subiecti, et talis est theologia quam philosophi prosequuntur quae alio nomine metaphysica dicitur." Cf. also *Ibid.,* 3m. Apparently, there is but one text suggesting the contrary: *In I Sent.,* Prol., q. 1, a. 3, sol. 1, where

A theology of wisdom

St. Thomas, the subject of a science is that whose causes and properties are sought in argumentation,[43] while the object embraces all the conclusions arrived at through demonstration.[44] It is quite evident that God enters the object of metaphysics as the first cause of being, but its subject remains being *qua* being.[45]

With being as its subject, metaphysics becomes fully wisdom in its attainment of the highest cause which is God: "Among the objects of the intellectual virtues wisdom's object is supreme; for wisdom considers the highest cause which is God."[46] What is most essential to wisdom is that it reach the heights and enter into contact with God. Brought by this demonstration of God to the summit of all reality, the wise man sees everything from God's point of view, objectively evaluated and ordered hierarchically in perspective: *Sapientis est ordinare*—it is proper to the

St. Thomas writes: "Metaphysica est divina quantum subiectum tantum." However, this is so obviously an exception to the position followed in his commentaries on Aristotle and Boethius, that if it is the original text, the latter works indicate a development in his thought. For the Chronological data concerning these works, see M. Grabmann, *Die Werke des hl. Thomas von Aquin* (Beiträge zur Geschichte der Philosophie und Theologie des Mittelalters, 1931), pp. 266, 269 & 312.

[43]"Hoc enim est subiectum in scientia cuius causas et passiones quaerimus." *In XII Libros Meta.*, Proem.

[44]Cf. *Summa* II-II, q. 1, a. 1, c. Subject and object may be distinguished further, for each can be considered as formal or material, but such distinctions are not necessary in the present discussion. See John of St. Thomas, *Curs. Theol.*, In I, q. 1, Disp. 2, a. 11 (Cited and commented upon by M. Glutz, *The Manner of Demonstrating*, pp. 41 ff.).

[45]As M. De Andrea, O.P., points out, for St. Thomas the subject of metaphysics is being *qua* being, expressed variously as *ens inquantum ens, ens commune, esse praedicamentale, esse finitum;* but God and the angels are part of metaphysics' object, because of the causal relation that obtains between the immaterial and material worlds. Cf. "Soggetto è oggetto della metafisica secondo S. Tommaso," *Angelicum,* 27 (1950) 165-95. As expressed by J. Maritain: "Le sujet de la métaphysique est l'analogue être considéré dans les analogues inférieurs ou nous l'appréhendons de fait, l'être créé et matériel commun aux dix prédicaments (c'est là que l'être nous apparaît avec les notes d'unité et de multiplicité, de puissance et d'acte . . .) Mais la même science qui a telle sorte de choses pour sujet porte aussi sur les causes de cette sorte de choses. C'est pourquoi la métaphysique débouche sur . . . les analogues supérieurs de l'être." *Les degrés,* p. 433, note 2.

[46]"Obiectum autem sapientiae praecellit inter obiecta omnium virtutum intellectualium: considerat enim causam altissimam quae Deus est." *Summa* I-II, q. 66, a. 5, c. Cf. also I, q. 1, a. 6, c; II-II, q. 45, a. 1, c.

wise man to order. All this is made possible because the primacy and universality of his subject permits the metaphysician to investigate the divine.[47]

It is obviously beyond our purpose here to present a complete structure of metaphysical wisdom. What is important is the recognition of being as the proper subject of metaphysics and the subsequent rise to the contemplation of highest causes. Complementing this central facet of human wisdom, there are various acts or functions, which either serve to effect or flow from that attainment of ultimate causality.

There is first the scientific investigation of being and its intrinsic principles, and the demonstration of God's existence and attributes—a sapiential function which is strictly scientific. Secondly, in virtue of penetrating the notion of being and the terms commonly associated with it, wisdom becomes authorized to judge, order, and defend first principles. St. Thomas suggests the relationship between this particular sapiential function and the wise man's contact with ultimate cause by saying: "To understand the meaning of being and non-being, of whole and part, and the other notions which follow upon being, from which as from terms the indemonstrable principles are constructed, is proper to wisdom, because common being is the proper effect of the highest cause, namely, God."[48] This aspect of metaphysical wisdom has been developed in the relatively modern field of epistemology, too often dissociated in the Wolffian tradition from its true place in metaphysics. Thirdly, the superior vantage point of the metaphysician gives him the right to judge and order the lower sciences, yet while respecting their individual autonomy.

---

[47]"(Philosophia prima) erit universalis et erit eius speculari de ente inquantum est ens et de eo quod quid est et de his quae sunt entis inquantum est ens; eadem enim est scientia primi entis et entis communis." *In VI Meta.*, lect. 1, no. 1170.

[48]"Cognoscere autem rationem entis et non entis, et totius et partis et aliorum quae consequuntur ad ens, ex quibus sicut ex terminis constituuntur principia indemonstrabilia, pertinet ad sapientiam: quia ens commune est proprius effectus causae altissimae, scilicet Dei." *Summa* I-II, q. 66, a. 5, ad 4.

These sapiential functions will be treated in more detail later in the chapter. For the moment, our problem concerns the determination of wisdom's principal or primary act, for although all the acts may be proper to wisdom, one should hold the primacy among the others. Is it the demonstrative discursus? Is it the judgment, evaluation, or defense of first principles? Or the authoritative judgment and use of the lesser sciences? Or perhaps none of these?

We have seen that what is essential to metaphysical wisdom is its contact with ultimate causes, a contact which is served by demonstration and is the basis for the other functions mentioned. Since the highest causes are really but one cause, God (though he could be considered as exemplary, efficient, and final cause and, therefore, in some sense plural), the metaphysician attains the divine. And because of the primacy of final causality, God is attained principally as ultimate final cause, as the end of all things. As shall be seen below, against this background of finality, because of the identification of end with good—here, necessarily of ultimate end with supreme good—the contact with God takes on a new dimension, it becomes contemplative. This is wisdom's primary act, contemplation.[49]

B. METAPHYSICS' PRIMARY ACT: CONTEMPLATION

In discussing metaphysical contemplation, four more or less distinct aspects will be examined: The act of contemplation itself in its relationship to God; the idea of end and, therefore,

---

[49]". . . habitum sapientiae cujus actus est felicitas contemplativa." *In II Sent.*, D. 41, q. 1, a. 1, sol.; "Contemplatio aliquando sumitur stricte pro actu intellectus divina meditantis. Et sic contemplatio est sapientiae actus." *In IV Sent.*, D. 15, q. 4, a. 1, q1a. 2, 1m; "Sapientia qua nunc contemplamur Deum . . ." *De Virt. in Comm.*, q. un., a. 12, 11m; "Sapientia est cognitio divinarum rerum unde pertinet ad contemplationem." *In I Cor.*, c. 1, lect. 3, no. 49; "Unde ad sapientiam per prius pertinet contemplatio divinorum, quae est visio principii." *Summa* II-II, q. 45, a. 3, ad 3 (Although the context here is the gift of wisdom, the thought expressed is evidently applicable to wisdom in any of its realizations). Cf. also *In III Sent.*, D. 35, q. 1, a. 2, sol. 3 and *In Boet. De Trin.*, q. 6, a. 4, obj. 3.

of happiness associated with that act; the affective element also present; and finally, the dimension of realism, one might even say, existentialism, in contemplation.

1. Metaphysical Contemplation and God

Contemplation in metaphysics must presuppose the proof and actual certitude of the existence of the first cause, for before the attainment of that ultimate cause metaphysics is but an inchoative wisdom.[50] In that prior demonstration the universe appears as the proper effect of God's causality, efficient and exemplary, as well as final, and by it the mind is made ready for the contemplative judgment which embraces God in his existence and the universe hierarchically ranged in relation to him. The *simplex intuitus veritatis*[51]—the simple vision of truth—characteristic of contemplation, is in contact with God, the first, highest, or ultimate cause, all terms associated with wisdom. St. Thomas writes:

> The contemplative considers other things insofar as they are ordered to the contemplation of God as to an end . . . Whence the word *contemplation* signifies that principal act by which God is contemplated in himself; while *speculation* refers rather to that act by which divine things are viewed in created things as in a mirror.[52]

The involvement of the total personality in contemplation, which will be shown below, demands that no object less than God, strictly speaking, be the proper object of contemplation. And only in wisdom, which guides the mind to the attainment of highest causes, is this possible.

The simplicity of contemplation's *simplex intuitus veritatis* implies more than an uncomplicated gaze at a single object. Metaphysical wisdom's contact with God implies also multi-

---

[50]Cf. M. D. Philippe, "Nature de l'acte de contemplation," p. 535.
[51]Cf. *Summa* II-II, q. 180, a. 3, ad 1 & a. 6, ad 2.
[52]"Contemplativus considerat alia inquantum ad Dei contemplationem ordinantur sicut in finem . . . Unde et nomen *contemplationis* significat illum actum principalem quo quis Deum in seipso contemplatur; sed *speculatio* magis nominat illum actum quo quis divina in rebus creatis quasi in speculo inspicit." *In III Sent.*, D. 35, q. 1, a. 2, sol. 3.

39

plicity, but a multiplicity which gives way to unity—the many become one, for the contemplative's grasp of highest causality gives birth immediately to the judgment and ordering of inferiors:

> In another way of contemplation (by way of judgment) the human mode moves from the simple vision of first principles and highest causes to judge and order inferiors. And this is realized by wisdom, which the Philosopher lists as an intellectual virtue because it is the wise man who orders—*sapientis est ordinare*.[53]

At the heart of this contemplation the distinction between the first two acts of the intellect, apprehension and judgment, becomes less important. Confronted by him whose essence is to exist, the intellect, essential in apprehension, existential in judgment, is perfected by an act presenting the two almost in synthesis. Although the structure of the intellect makes forever impossible a complete identification of apprehension and judgment, the judgment of God's existence is unique in approaching it, for his essence is his existence.[54] This supreme intellectual act finds its completion, integral rather than essential, in the judgment of everything else as related to God as highest cause; this is the primary meaning of the adage: *Sapientis est ordinare*.[55] In this way the contemplation of the philosopher resolves the unintelligibility of the many in a simple grasp of intelligible

[53]"In alia autem via contemplationis modus humanus est ut ex simplici inspectione primorum principiorum et altissimarum causarum homo de inferioribus judicet et ordinet. Et hoc fit per sapientiam quam ponit Philosophus intellectualem virtutem, quia *sapientis est ordinare*." *Ibid.,* D. 34, q. 1, a. 2, sol.

[54]All this may seem somewhat oversimplified, because God's essence is really hidden from us. What remains true, however, is that the contemplative judgment regarding God's existence is something vitally unique.

[55]"(La sagesse philosophique) ne peut créer, mais simplement découvrir et contempler l'ordre et la hiérarchie établis par Dieu, Sagesse incréée. C'est précisément cette découverte et cette contemplation qu'on désigne quand, parlant sur le plan philosophique, on dit: 'Sapientis est ordinare.' On voit alors que, si juger, c'est apprécier les choses selon leur nature et leur valeur, donc d'après leurs rapports mutuels de supériorité et d'infériorité, de domination et de dépendance, d'utilisation et d'utilité, 'ordonner' sera un acte impliqué dans ce jugement." J. Peghaire, *Intellectus et ratio*, pp. 165-66.

unity—its expression: *Videre omnia in conspectu Dei*—to see all things as God sees them.

2. *Metaphysical Contemplation and Finality*

The idea of order contained in contemplative vision suggests immediately the notion of end or final cause, the inevitable rule of all order. To possess a universal view of reality, ranged hierarchically in relationship to the supreme cause, requires an awareness of that cause as *final*. St. Thomas writes:

> . . . it is the wise man who orders: the ordering of things is possible only with a knowledge of those things in mutual inter-relations as well as in reference to something above and beyond them, their end. To know these mutual interrelations and proportions is proper to an intelligence; and to judge of things in the light of the highest cause is proper to wisdom. Therefore, all ordering must be realized by the wisdom of some intelligent being.[56]

The priority and posteriority involved in order demand some principle as criterion, according to which things can be judged in their relation to one another.[57] In wisdom's object the order contemplated is that of the entire universe; its criterion, God as highest cause. Wisdom's insight penetrates God as the principle of all things, as ultimate efficient cause, and, therefore, embraces the totality of the real as proceeding from God.

---

[56]". . . ordinare sapientis est: ordinatio aliquorum fieri non potest nisi per cognitionem habitudinis et proportionis ordinatorum ad invicem et ad aliquid altius eius, quod est finis eorum: ordo enim aliquorum ad invicem est propter ordinem ad finem. Cognoscere autem habitudines et proportiones aliquorum ad invicem est solius habentis intellectum; iudicare de aliquibus per causam altissimam sapientiae est. Et sic oportet quod omnis ordinatio per sapientiam alicuius intelligentis fiat." *Cont. Gent.*, II, 24, in medio. ". . . sapientis est ordinare. Cuius ratio est quia sapientia est potissima perfectio rationis, cuius proprium est cognoscere ordinem . . . ordinem tamen unius rei ad aliam cognoscere est solius intellectus aut rationis. Invenitur autem duplex ordo in rebus. Unus quidem partium alicuius totius seu alicuius multitudinis ad invicem . . . Alius est ordo rerum in finem. Et hic ordo est principalior quam primus." *In I Eth.*, lect. 1, no. 1. See also *Cont. Gent.*, I, 1.

[57]"Cum enim principium importet ordinem quemdam ad alia necesse est invenire principium in omnibus in quibus est ordo." *In Joannem*, c. 1, lect. 1, no. 34.

However, its contact with him as ultimate final cause provides properly the basis for the vision of order: *Finis est causa causarum.*[58] God seen as the end of everything else permits the wise man to range reality in order under him.

With the introduction of ultimate final cause, the nature of this knowledge we call wisdom takes on a new dimension. God is no longer viewed simply as the highest truth to be known; he becomes at the same time the supreme good to be loved. This identification of *prima veritas* and *summum bonum* in its most perfect object colors the purely speculative values of metaphysics with affective tones unknown in lower disciplines. Wisdom's grasp of God as principle and end, as creator and happiness, becomes far more personal. Here the object of the knowledge itself engages the individual, not merely the knowledge. If it is true that Greek philosophy or pagan wisdom in any of its forms is interested in contemplation merely as an act perfecting the one who contemplates, and not as the attainment of the infinitely desirable Person of God, it is because, as wisdom, it remains incomplete. The true metaphysician must realize that the final end of all things is also his own proper end—he cannot remain indifferent.

Closely related with what has been said above is the association of human happiness with metaphysical wisdom's contemplative act. Suggested in the text, "The contemplation of divine truth is the end of all human life,"[59] this truth is adapted to the human situation as St. Thomas writes:

> Wisdom considers the very object of happiness, the supreme intelligible being. And if wisdom's consideration of its object were perfect, there would be perfect happiness in the act of wisdom. But because in this life the act of wisdom is imperfect with respect to its principal object, that act is a certain beginning or participation of future happiness.[60]

[58]*In V. Meta.*, lect. 3, no. 782. Cf. also *In I Post. Anal.*, lect. 16; *Summa* I, q. 105, a. 5, c; I-II, q. 1, a. 2, c.
[59]"Contemplatio divinae veritatis est finis totius humanae vitae." *Summa* II-II, q. 180, a. 4, c.
[60]"Sapientia considerat ipsum obiectum felicitatis quod est altissimum intelligibile. Et si quidem esset perfecta consideratio sapientiae respectu

On earth wisdom's act of contemplating God is for us the beginning of our happiness, which will be realized perfectly in heaven. Even metaphysics, as the habit of philosophical contemplation, brings with it this inchoative happiness in a manner consonant with its nature. For this reason, the contemplation proper to metaphysical wisdom cannot help but engage the whole personality—the object contemplated is the ultimate end of the individual metaphysician to be attained on earth and in heaven; now in imperfect, later in perfect, vision.

3. Metaphysical Contemplation and Affectivity

Essentially, the affective dimension in natural wisdom comes into being in the awareness of God as end or final cause. Less universal disciplines present the knower not with an end but with an object to be viewed in disinterested detachment. Though a mathematician, for example, may be ardently attached to the mathematical act itself as a type of knowing, he can never engage himself affectively to a formal quantity. This is not the case in metaphysics. Here, the object itself, as the ultimate end and happiness of the individual, can and should evoke an affective response—the truly wise man, the perfect metaphysician, cannot remain in detached disinterestedness. He is immediately engaged, involved, committed.[61] God as contemplated in metaphysics cannot remain a pure object. The presence of infinite personality, in whom "the supremely desirable is identified with

sui obiecti, esset perfecta felicitas in actu sapientiae. Sed quia actus sapientiae in hac vita est imperfectus respectu principalis obiecti quod est Deus; ideo actus sapientiae est quaedam inchoatio seu participatio futurae felicitatis." *Summa* I-II, q. 66, a. 5, ad 2. Concerning the association of happiness with wisdom's contemplation, see also *In X Eth.*, lect. 10-13, passim; *In III Sent.*, D. 35, q. 1, a. 2, sol. 3; *In Boet. De Trin.*, q. 6, a. 4, obj. 3; *Cont. Gent.*, III, 25 & 37; *Summa* I-II, q. 57, a. 1, ad 2; q. 66, a. 3, ad 1.

[61]In this context there is an interesting passage written by J.-H. Nicolas, O.P.: "Si la métaphysique est essentiellement la prise de possession par l'intelligence de l'être en sa réalité totale, il est clair que de la connaissance métaphysique naîtra d'une part un mouvement d'amour et d'adoration où l'âme s'engagera à fond et d'autre part un besoin de prolonger cette intuition intellectuelle pour pénétrer toutes les richessses de l'être qu'elle nous livre." in "L'intuition de l'être et le premier principe," *Revue thomiste*, 47 (1947), pp. 132-33.

the supremely intelligible,"[62] introduces the metaphysician into a world where the cold and arid atmosphere of an indifferent intellectualism is charged with new life and warmth and meaning. All this may belie the popular impression of the philosopher as impassive, detached, unengaged, and of philosophy as dry and uninteresting; but this is precisely the caricature drawn of wisdom of which we have spoken earlier. Happily, it is but a caricature.

In analyzing affectivity in contemplation, St. Thomas is careful to distinguish between the love of the object contemplated and the love of contemplation itself.[63] Either of these loves can prompt one to the act of contemplation and provide the source for the corresponding joy that results. In the personal involvement of which we have been speaking, the initial and terminal affectivity must embrace the object contemplated, God as final cause, rather than the subjective perfection of the metaphysician.[64] The contemplative confrontation of the wise man with the presence of him who is man's final end necessarily opens on the world of affectivity. As far as possible in the natural order there is realized in the metaphysician the "ultimate perfection of the contemplative life: that divine truth not only be known but that it also be loved."[65]

[62]M. D. Philippe, "Nature de l'acte de contemplation," p. 541—paraphrased from Aristotle, *Metaphysics*, Bk. 12, chap. 7 (1072 a 27).

[63]Cf. *Summa* II-II, q. 180, a. 1, c; *In III Sent.*, D. 35, q. 1, a. 2, sol. 1.

[64]It is true that ordinarily the contemplation of the saints is opposed to that of the philosophers on the basis of this very distinction, interest in the object contemplated being denied to philosophers. Cf. St. Albert the Great, *De Adhaerendo Deo*, (Ed., Borgnet. Paris: Vives, 1898) XXXVII, 532. St. Thomas holds much the same position in *In III Sent.*, D. 35, q. 1, a. 2, sol. 1, but his point of departure, as love of self in the case of the philosopher, seems rather a judgment of paganism than a denial of metaphysics' interest in God.

[65]"Ultima perfectio contemplativae vitae: ut scilicet non solum divina veritas videatur sed etiam ut ametur." *Summa* II-II, q. 180, a. 7, ad 1. In another text St. Thomas is speaking *ex professo* of contemplation proper to the gift of wisdom, but his thought seems applicable proportionately to every form of true contemplation, acquired or infused. He writes: "Unde ipsius (sapientiae) actus videtur hic et in futuro divina amata contemplari . . ." *In III Sent.*, D. 35, q. 2, a. 1, sol. 3.

With the awareness of God as personal and lovable, metaphysical contemplation's initial affectivity becomes the love of the object contemplated, not merely of contemplation itself. Similarly, the joy and delight experienced, the terminal affectivity, stem from the object and not from the intellectual act as such.[66] Here, we find re-emphasized the association of contemplation and happiness. The individual, transcending the temporal and the transitory, attains in that most perfect act of man's highest faculty God, known and loved in contemplative vision. The resultant joy is but the ultimate fruit of metaphysical wisdom.[67] Admittedly, the comprehension is slight, for God is seen as mirrored in created effects; but the inevitable affective involvement in this most excellent of objects gives birth to a joy surpassing the essential inadequacy of the contact. St. Thomas explains:

> "The lover finds more delight in the least knowledge of the one loved than in a comprehensive knowledge of other things" (Aristotle, *On the Parts of Animals*, a. 5, 644 b 24ff.). And therefore, as he remarks, the little we are able to know regarding separated substances is more desirable and more delightful than whatever knowledge we may have of other things.[68]

---

[66]Cf. *Summa* II-II, q. 180, a. 7, c.

[67]"Regard pénétrant, immobile, unique, plein, la contemplation est aussi accompagnée de joie. Elle est même le seul acte de l'intelligence qui, par nature, implique une note affective. Avec elle on semble dominer la distinction entre l'esprit et le coeur. 'Sapientis est sapida scientia' dit St. Augustin. La sagesse est toujours suave. Elle n'a plus la sécheresse et la froideur de la science. Elle est pleine d'onction. L'intelligence a enfin trouvé l'objet qui lui convient, qui lui ressemble; et cette similitude, cette parenté la remplissent de joie . . . En lui (Dieu) les désirs de l'intelligence comme ceux du coeur sont comblés et il peut seul donner à la contemplation les caractères de joie et d'épanouissement qui semblent être son apanage." T. Philippe, "Spéculation métaphysique et contemplation chrétienne," *Angelicum*, 14 (1937), p. 224.

[68]"'Amans in parva comprehensione amati magis delectatur quam in magna aliorum comprehensione' (Aristotle, I *Part. Anim.* a. 5, 644b24sq.). Et ideo, ut ipse dicit, illud parum quod de substantiis separatis cognoscere possumus plus desideratur et delectatur quam quidquid de aliis rebus cognoscimus." *In III Sent.*, D. 35, q. 2, a. 2, sol. 2 (the reference to Aristotle should read: 644 b 35 ff.). Cf. also: *In I Meta.*, lect. 3, no. 60; *Cont. Gent.*, I, 5 & 8; *Summa* I-II, q. 66, a. 5, ad 3.

A theology of wisdom

What has already been said concerning affectivity in metaphysical contemplation is not an attempt to make wisdom something essentially affective. Those who held that position in virtue of the etymological maxim, *sapientia est scientia sapida,* were refuted by St. Thomas, who simply pointed out that the argument does not hold in Greek nor in other languages besides the Latin.[69] What remains true, however, and what seems to have been too often overlooked, is that metaphysical wisdom, in attaining the supremely intelligible, who is at once the supremely lovable and desirable, must be open to affective overtones.

4. Metaphysical Contemplation and Realism

In re-evaluating metaphysical wisdom's contemplative act, "essentially a completely simple view of God,"[70] the dimension of affectivity of which we have been speaking introduces a profound realism otherwise not apparent. In the contemplative vision of God as man's end and happiness, intellect and will seem to transcend their inherent dualism and become one in the higher unity of the personality. Knowledge and love, too often divorced and made to oppose one another, appear united in perfect harmony.[71] As person confronts Person and the identification of Infinite Truth with Supreme Goodness is discovered, the fortress world of intellect can no longer remain aloof and untouched. The subdued tones of its ideal, essential character are brought to life and made rich by the affective coloring of realist, existential tones. The individual as a whole is involved in wisdom. He is engaged, committed to God as personal and present, infinitely knowable, infinitely lovable and attained in

[69]See *In III Sent.,* D. 35, q. 2, a. 1, qla. 3, 1m and *Summa* II-II, q. 45, a. 2, ad 2.

[70]J. Peghaire, *Intellectus et ratio,* p. 296: ". . . en effet la contemplation est essentiellement une vue toute simple de Dieu."

[71]"Les philosophies rationalistes posent toutes inévitablement un divorce mortel entre la connaissance et l'amour. L'existentialisme thomiste les accorde et les unit, et fonde l'amour sur l'intelligence et fortifie l'intelligence par l'amour." J. Maritain, "L'humanisme de St. Thomas d'Aquin," *Medieval Studies,* 3 (1941), p. 177.

contemplation. Metaphysical wisdom's contemplation cannot, therefore, be a disinterested regard of an object seen merely as another object; its contact with highest truth as ultimate cause is far more living, an experience in becoming whole, in fulfillment. As St. Thomas writes: "The end of contemplation, as contemplation, is truth alone, but as associated with the notion of life contemplation takes on an affective character."[72]

In the moments of contemplation the individual, in a certain sense, attains his end, as his soul reaches beyond the order of means, the realm of the restless and too often rootless present, to rest in the eternity of God. Nothing could be more realist or more existential in the true sense of *engagement* than this contemplation. It is wisdom's primary act.[73]

III. The Functions of Metaphysical Wisdom

Because wisdom is a potential whole it embraces a plurality of acts or functions. To speak, therefore, of the act of wisdom would be ambiguous were the phrase not immediately qualified. It does seem true, however, that contemplation could be called simply the act of wisdom, that is, if wisdom's other acts were restricted to being called functions. One does not speak of

[72]"Finis contemplationis, inquantum contemplatio, est veritas tantum, sed secundum quod contemplatio accipit *rationem vitae,* sic induit rationem affectati et boni." *In III Sent.,* D. 35, q. 1, a. 2, q1a. 1, 1m.

[73]What we have written in the preceding pages may suggest a more explicit Platonic flavor in Thomistic wisdom, as pointed out by two German authors, J. Lenz and J. Hirschberger (see chap. 1, note 63). As the latter writes: "Vielleicht hat eine innere Wahlverwandtschaft den christlichen Theologen und Philosophen dahin gedrängt; denn jetzt können Metaphysik und Ethik sich wieder verbinden; erstes Prinzip und letztes Ziel allen Seins fallen wieder zusammen mit dem summum bonum; der Weise hat nicht mehr bloss zu erkennen, sondern auch zu urteilen und zu handeln." in "Quod sit officium sapientis," p. 37. Both writers point up the essential "Lebenswert" of wisdom as involving the whole man. However as M. D. Philippe remarks, while Plato is concerned only with formal cause, Aristotle discovers the primacy and consequent supremacy of final cause. (Cf. "La sagesse selon Aristote," pp. 373-74). As we have seen, the affective involvement is rooted precisely in that awareness of God as final cause, as man's perfection and happiness. Therefore, rather than reduce St. Thomas's dependence on Aristotle in favor of Plato, it seems more correct to see a double dependence, with Plato's influence coming to St. Thomas through Aristotle.

contemplation as a function—it is an act *par excellence*. The other acts, though all essential to wisdom, are properly functions subordinate to wisdom's act of contemplation. From a literary as well as from a philosophical or theological point of view contemplation could not be termed a function—it is indeed *the act of wisdom*.

While these remarks might offer a basis for speaking of contemplation simply as the act of wisdom, in order to avoid any ambiguity the addition of the word, primary, has been made. But it should be remembered that contemplation is not just another act of wisdom, even one that is first among equals. It enjoys an absolute ascendancy. For this reason, in each of the three chapters devoted to the distinct wisdoms of metaphysics, theology, and the gift, contemplation is treated in connection with the respective natures of these wisdoms. The other sapiential acts, the so-called functions of wisdom, are discussed independently.

In the present section our interest turns to the functions of metaphysical wisdom and, first of all, to the function of demonstration which justifies metaphysics as science and prepares the ascent to the act of contemplation.

A. METAPHYSICAL WISDOM AND DEMONSTRATION

1. "It belongs to the wise man to possess demonstrative knowledge concerning certain things, i.e., concerning the first causes of beings."[74] Without the demonstration of God's existence there can be no human wisdom, for there is no knowledge of highest cause; in wisdom's contemplative judgment and ordination of all things, the criterion, the point of reference, is God as ultimate final cause.[75] But metaphysics' demonstrative function does not end here. After God's existence as the exemplary, efficient and final cause of all things is reached through *quia* demonstration

[74]"Ad sapientem pertinet quod habeat demonstrationem de aliquibus rebus, idest de primis causis entium." *In VI Eth.*, lect. 5, no. 1177.
[75]". . . sapientia quae considerat altissimas causas. Unde convenienter iudicat et ordinat de omnibus: quia iudicium perfectum et universale haberi non potest nisi per resolutionem ad primas causas." *Summa* I-II, q. 57, a. 2, c.

(from effect to proper cause), there remains the investigation of his attributes. In this phase the metaphysician, using for the most part *propter quid* demonstration (from proper cause to effect)[76], elaborates the various perfections which, though identified in God, must be conceived independently by the human mind. When this particular process involves divine perfections participated by creatures, the metaphysician employs the three recognized modes of predicating divine names: *affirmatively* (the created perfection really exists in God, its cause), *negatively* (the imperfection of the created analogate cannot belong to God) and *eminently* (the perfection in God implies the dimension of infinity).[77]

It is true that there are demonstrations in metaphysics prior to that of God's existence and his attributes, the demonstration of the properties of being, for example; however, the demonstrations touching upon highest cause are of greater importance from the point of view of wisdom.

2. Having seen that contemplation is the primary act of wisdom, it might be well to clarify here exactly what is meant, for in a sense the mind perfected by science also contemplates: "All science attains its perfection in vision."[78] Because of this it may seem arbitrary to restrict the act of contemplation to wisdom, yet there is a solid basis for that restriction. The discursus of science, the movement from principles to conclusions (*via inventionis*) and the resolution to principles (*via iudicii*), terminates in a seeing, a contemplation of a sort wherein the conclusion is viewed bathed in the light of its principles. In lesser sciences, however, the conclusion remains but an object, it is never an end. Such an object cannot engage the entire personality (a characteristic of contemplation), nor does it serve to range reality hierarchically in perspective, as is the case in wisdom's attainment of ultimate final cause. For this reason,

[76]Cf. the text of John of St. Thomas cited above, note 31.
[77]Cf. *De. Pot.*, q. 7, a. 5, 2m and its commentary in C. Journet, *Connaissance et inconnaissance de Dieu* (Paris: Egloff, 1943), pp. 104-19, passim.
[78]"Omnis scientia in visione rei perficitur." *De Ver.*, q. 14, a. 9, c.

we speak of science's essential act as demonstration, that of wisdom as contemplation. It is true that the phrase, *scientia est conclusionum* (science is of conclusions), may fail to point up the vital circular movement in the return to principles and the consequent deeper understanding of the principles in an act of quasi-contemplation.[79] But this does not mean that science has the same concern with principles or with ultimates, proper to wisdom.[80]

As a final observation in considering metaphysics' properly scientific function, the resolution to principles is more profoundly meaningful than in the lower sciences, because the depths of the principles have been uncovered by another of metaphysics' sapiential functions, which will be our concern in the following section.

B. METAPHYSICAL WISDOM AND FIRST PRINCIPLES

1. "Wisdom is a certain science concerning principles."[81] But before investigating the function of metaphysical wisdom concerning principles, we must make certain exactly which principles are involved. Though the text just cited might seem to fit the present context, it does not concern the principles which wisdom is expected to judge, evaluate, order and defend. The supposition of the word "principles" points to the causal principles of things, ultimately to the unique principle of all reality, God as highest cause. But God is wisdom's concern in its contemplative act. Here, the principles in question are the indemonstrable

[79]The criticisms of theology as science which will be discussed in the following chapter are based upon a too literal interpretation of this phrase. Concerning science's necessary return to principles in the resolution of conclusions see the following texts: *In III Sent.*, D. 23, q. 2, a. 2, sol. 3; D. 24, a. 2, sol. 1; D. 35, q. 1, a. 2, sol. 2; *In I Post. Anal.*, lect. 1, no. 6; *In Boet. De Trin.*, q. 6, a. 1, c. (ad 1am quaest. et ad 3am quaest.); *De Ver.*, q. 11, a. 1, 13m; q. 14, a. 1, c.; q. 15, a. 1, c.; *De Div. Nom.*, c. 7, lect. 2, no. 713; *Summa* I, q. 14, a. 7, c.; q. 79, a. 8, c.; a. 12, c.

[80]The argumentation in this paragraph finds a parallel in the following words of E. Gilson: "Si la contemplation est la forme la plus haute de la vie humaine, c'est à condition qu'elle porte sur l'objet dont la connaissance est la fin de cette vie." *Le thomisme*, p. 13.

[81]"Sapientia est scientia quaedam circa principia." *In XI Meta.*, lect. 1, no. 2146.

first principles of being and knowledge, for example, the principles of contradiction, identity, efficient, exemplary, and final causality. When attempting to name metaphysics' function regarding these principles, one is easily lost in such words as interpretative, evaluative, judicative, explicative, definitional, expositive, elucidative, defensive, none of which seems a happy choice to express exactly what is meant. However, the principles do stand in need of being explained or interpreted, ordered according to their importance, and defended; and this complex operation is proper to metaphysical wisdom.

The right or duty of metaphysics to concern itself with principles is not simply an arbitrary choice made by the wise man to set himself up as judge and defender. Its basis is far more realistic. St. Thomas writes:

> The truth and knowledge of the indemonstrable principles depend upon the meaning of the terms; for given the knowledge of the nature of whole and of part it is immediately known that the whole is greater than the part. To understand however the meaning of being and non-being, of whole and part, and the other notions which follow upon being, from which as from terms the indemonstrable principles are constructed, is proper to wisdom, because common being is the proper effect of the highest cause, namely, God. And therefore wisdom uses the indemonstrable principles held by understanding not only in drawing conclusions from them, as do other sciences, but also in judging them and in disputing with those who would deny them.[82]

[82]"Veritas et cognitio principiorum indemonstrabilium dependet ex ratione terminorum: cognito enim quid est totum et quid est pars, statim cognoscitur quod omne totum est maius sua parte. Cognoscere autem rationem entis et non entis, et totius et partis, et aliorum quae consequuntur ad ens, ex quibus sicut ex terminis constituuntur principia indemonstrabilia, pertinet ad sapientiam: quia ens commune est proprius effectus causae altissimae, scilicet Dei. Et ideo sapientia non solum utitur principiis indemonstrabilibus, quorum est intellectus, concludendo ex eis sicut aliae scientiae; sed etiam iudicando de eis, et disputando contra negantes." *Summa* I-II, q. 66, a. 5, ad 4. "(Oportet) quod sapientia verum dicat circa ipsa principia prima: non quod demonstret ea: sed inquantum ad sapientes pertinet notificare communia, puta totius et partis, aequale et inaequale, et alia huiusmodi, quibus cognitis principia demum innotescunt." *In VI Eth.*, lect. 5, no. 1182. Cf. also *In III Meta.*, lect. 5, no. 392; *In XI Meta.*, lect. 1, no. 2151.

A theology of wisdom

We saw earlier that wisdom in a sense subsumes into itself the lesser intellectual habits of understanding and science—it touches directly upon principles and conclusions. Here, we see precisely what justifies that authoritative concern with principles and its consequent supremacy over understanding. The metaphysician's penetration of being and those notions immediately associated with being means that his habit of understanding is no longer a simple assent to first principles, but a far more profound grasp of their content.[83]

2. Of equal importance in metaphysical wisdom's interpretative judgment and evaluation of principles, and another instance of the maxim, *sapientis est ordinare,* is the ordering of the principles among themselves and their reduction to one which is primary:

> Wisdom in a certain sense includes understanding, for while it reasons about ultimates by using principles it also orders the principles themselves by reducing them to one which is primary and it defends them against those who deny them.[84]

The one principle which stands above the others, to which all must ultimately be resolved, is that of contradiction, "the absolutely first principle: it is impossible that the same thing be and not be."[85]

3. With the interpretation of the principles and their ordered resolution to the principle of contradiction as supreme, the

83Cf. the exposition of this sapiential function in C. Williams, O.P., *De Multiplici Virtutum Forma* (Rome, 1954), pp. 21-41. Wisdom's superiority is clearly established.

84"(Sapientia) quodammodo comprehendit ipsum (intellectum) secundum quod ex principiis negotiatur circa altissima et difficillima, et de his etiam quodammodo ordinat, inquantum reducit omnia ad unum principium, et ejus est disputare contra negantes ipsa." *In III Sent.,* D. 35, q. 2, a. 1, q1a. 1, 1m. John of St. Thomas remarks: "Quomodo ergo sapientia potest reflectere super sua principia, cum illa sint communissima et universalissima, et sic non possint ad altiora principia reduci, respondetur quod etiam ipsa sapientia habet plura principia quorum unum est universalius alio et constat terminis magis notis quoad nos . . ." *Curs. Theol.,* In I-II, Disp. XVI, a. 3, no. 6 (Vives, VI, 465).

85". . . maxime primum principium, scilicet quod impossibile est idem esse et non esse." *In III Meta.,* lect. 5, no. 392. See also *In IV Meta.,* lect. 6, no. 600.

sapiential function under discussion moves to the defense of that absolutely first principle. In defending the other principles, the metaphysician must first reduce them to contradiction, which in turn comes under attack.[86]

In refuting the position of one who denies the principle of contradiction, the metaphysician takes as his point of departure the words of his opponent. If the words used by the opponent are given any meaning at all, he is applying the principle he claims to deny—he does not identify an affirmation with a negation; therefore, he is in contradiction with himself. In case the opponent does not admit his words have a determined sense, if his "yes" is equally "no," his "no" equally "yes," there can be no discussion:

> . . . it can be shown that it is impossible that the same thing be and not be, but only if he who from some doubt denies the principle actually says something, that is, signifies something by his words. If indeed he says nothing, it is ridiculous to seek a reason from one who uses no reason in speaking.[87]

This defense by way of negative demonstration is reinforced by pointing up the impossibilities which result from a denial of the principle. Among others indicated by Aristotle and restated by St. Thomas, are the suppression of all signification—a word would mean nothing; the destruction of diversity—everything would be equally everything else and therefore nothing could exist; the elimination of all thought and expression and truth and falsity—every statement would be both true and false; the reduction to impossibility of all choice—since nothing would

[86]The defense itself is found presented in Aristotle, *Metaphysics*, Bk. IV, chaps. 3-8 with St. Thomas's commentary. For an analysis of this defensive negative demonstration, cf. M. D. Philippe, *Initiation à la philosophie d'Aristote*, pp. 121-26 and "La sagesse selon Aristote," pp. 350-56. For other texts concerning human wisdom's defensive function, see: *In Boet. De Trin.*, q. 2, a. 2, 4m; *In VI Eth.*, lect. 5, no. 1182; *In III Meta.*, lect. 5, no. 392; *Summa* I, q. 1, a. 8, c; I-II, q. 66, a. 5, ad 4.

[87]". . . ostendi potest quod impossibile sit idem esse et non esse. Sed solum si ille qui ex aliqua dubitatione negat illud principium, *dicit aliquid,* idest aliquid nomine significat. Si vero nihil dicit, derisibile est quaerere aliquam rationem ad illum qui nulla utitur ratione loquendo." *In IV Meta.*, lect. 6, no. 608.

be good or bad, or everything would be both good and bad, the individual would remain forever indifferent and undecided.[88] This is the picture painted of the human situation without the principle of contradiction founding its ontological, logical, and ethical worlds. Here, the defense rests, and with it the discussion of metaphysics' concern for principles.

C. METAPHYSICAL WISDOM AND THE OTHER SCIENCES

1. In studying metaphysical wisdom's relationship to other sciences, we meet a third instance of the maxim, *sapientis est ordinare,* a function best signified by the word, *architectonic.*[89] The vantage point of wisdom, realized in its contact with God as highest cause, grants it certain privileges of judgment and direction over the lower sciences. Basically, the argumentation establishing the validity of wisdom's contemplative judgment (all things ordered to God as ultimate final cause) is also valid here, where the lesser sciences are ordered to wisdom as to their end. Among the highest causes considered by wisdom is highest final cause. "Hence it belongs to metaphysics to consider the ultimate and universal end of all things. And so, all the other sciences are ordered to it as to their end."[90] As we saw earlier, order and the judgment it presupposes depend entirely upon the awareness of end or final cause, and the extent of the privilege depends upon the more or less ultimate character of the final cause considered. Since metaphysical wisdom touches ultimate finality, its supremacy is unquestioned, and its judgment and direction become universal.[91] Were this

---

[88]Cf. Aristotle, *Metaphysics,* Bk. IV, chap. 4 (1006 a 29—1008 b 32) and St. Thomas, *In IV Meta.,* lect. 7-9, nos. 612-58.

[89]Cf. *In I Meta.,* lect. 2, no. 50; *Cont. Gent.,* III, 25; *Summa* I-II, q. 66, a. 5, c.

[90]"Unde oportet quod haec scientia (metaphysica) consideret ultimum et universalem finem omnium. Et sic omnes aliae scientiae in eam ordinantur sicut in finem." *In I Meta.,* lect. 3, no. 59. See also *Proemium,* in init.

[91]". . . sapientia quae considerat altissimas causas. Unde convenienter iudicat et ordinat de omnibus." *Summa* I-II, q. 57, a. 2, c.; "(Sapientia) considerat causam altissimam quae Deus est. Et quia per causam iudicatur de effectu, et per causam superiorem de causis inferioribus; inde est

truth more clearly recognized, contemporary problems regarding the integration of academic curricula would no longer plague so many present-day educational institutions.

2. When referring to the metaphysician's role as judge of the lesser sciences, we must be careful to guard intact the autonomy of each science within its particular field. "Metaphysics, which orders the other sciences, considers being taken absolutely; the other sciences, however, study being according to some particular determination."[92] Because this is so, metaphysics does not share the same degree of abstraction nor the same methodology as the lower sciences and, therefore, has no right to judge within the science itself, except in relation to principles proper to metaphysics:

> In this manner (as architectonic and preceptive) first philosophy is related to the other speculative sciences, for upon her these other sciences depend. They receive their principles from her as well as direction in defending those principles against those who deny them.[93]

Each science, though dependent upon metaphysics for its principles and their defense, remains independent within the particular sphere of its inquiry.

3. A final aspect of wisdom's relation to other sciences is its right to use them in its own development. All human knowledge has no other purpose than to lead ultimately to knowledge

---

quod sapientia habet iudicium de omnibus aliis virtutibus intellectualibus; et eius est ordinare omnes; et ipsa est quasi architectonica respectu omnium." *Ibid.*, q. 66, a. 5, c.; "Illa scientia se habet ad alias ut principalis sive ut architectonica ad servilem sive ad famulantem quae considerat causam finalem cuius causa agenda sunt singula . . . Sed praedicta scientia (metaphysica) maxime considerat causam finalem rerum omnium . . . ergo est principalis sive architectonica omnium aliarum (scientiarum)." *In I Meta.*, lect. 2, no. 50.

92"Metaphysica, quae est ordinativa aliarum (scientiarum), considerat rationem entis absolute; aliae vero secundum determinationem aliquam." *In II Sent.*, D. 3, q. 3, a. 2, sol. See also *In VI Meta.*, lect. 1, no. 1147.

93"Hoc autem modo (ut architectonica et praeceptiva) se habet philosophia prima ad alias scientias speculativas nam ab ipsa omnes aliae dependent, utpote ab ipsa accipientes sua principia et directionem contra negantes principia." *Cont. Gent.*, III, 25. Cf. also *In VI Eth.*, lect. 6, no. 1184 and *In XI Meta.*, lect. 1, no. 2151.

of God—"The ultimate perfection of the human intellect is divine truth; other truths perfect the intellect as ordered toward divine truth."[94]—and this sublime objective means simply that all the lower disciplines must serve the good of wisdom.[95]

To judge, to order, to direct, to rule, to use—all these are contained within the architectonic function of metaphysical wisdom, summed up as a third realization of the proposition: *Sapientis est ordinare.* We saw first wisdom's ordering all things in contemplation, then its ordering of principles; here we see its prerogative justified in relation to the lower sciences.[96]

D. THE INCOMPLETENESS OF METAPHYSICAL WISDOM

In this final consideration, we touch neither a function nor an act of wisdom, but rather one of its characteristics. Throughout the entire structure of metaphysics, the mind is confronted by the mystery of being, in whose soundless depths is hidden the meaning of existence. What does it mean to exist, to be? Then, as the wise man ascends to contemplate the first cause of all created being, he is faced with the incomparably greater mystery of God. In the face of this mystery the knowledge of purely human wisdom is left radically and tragically incomplete.

The term of metaphysics is realized as the wise man "touches the final causality of the supreme separated substance, sov-

[94]"Ultima perfectio humani intellectus est veritas divina; aliae autem veritates perficiunt intellectum in ordine ad veritatem divinam." *Summa* II-II, q. 180, a. 4, ad 4. "Omnis cognitio veritatis quae nobis necessaria est de aliis rebus, referenda est ad cognitionem veritatis divinae . . . Et ideo omnis cognitio veritatis pertinet ad sapientiam." *In Psal. XLIV,* in init.; "Est ergo cognitio divina finis ultimus omnis humanae cognitionis et operationis." *Cont. Gent.,* III, 25.

[95]"Metaphysica, quae est omnibus (scientiis) superior, utitur his quae in aliis scientiis sunt probata." *In Boet. De Trin.,* q. 2, a. 3, 7m.

[96]A fourth instance of *sapientis est ordinare* in the natural order belongs to prudence (sapientia viro), which orders human acts to their proper end. Cf. *Summa* II-II, q. 47, a. 2, ad 1. However, because metaphysical wisdom as such does not concern itself with means but only with ultimate end, this particular ordering stands outside its competence and beyond our discussion. In the higher wisdoms, theology and the gift, we shall see that there is a concern for means not found in the natural wisdom of first philosophy.

ereignly desirable and lovable."[97] But because God is attained
not in himself but as reflected in his creation, he remains
unknown from within.[98] Metaphysical wisdom's contemplative
act, though true knowledge, is wrapped in mystery and best
expressed in negation, for the infinite cannot be contained in
finite concepts.[99] It is not the divine nature in its infinite intelligibility, which creates the necessity of this negation, but rather
our mode of conception. And yet, to know that God escapes
the limitation of our concepts is really to know him. Paradoxically, negation becomes affirmation. At the highest point
of natural human knowledge, therefore, we arrive at the contemplation of God as unknown and are brought to realize that
we know God best, when we know we do not know him.[100]
Here, it becomes apparent that "the great joy of the philosopher
is to be convinced that God surpasses all knowledge, that in an
absolute sense he is unknowable. The metaphysician is not able
to rest elsewhere; every other joy has necessarily something
limited for its object; and that joy which comes from the mystery
is already at its level a foretaste of eternal happiness."[101] This

[97] M. D. Philippe, *Initiation à la philosophie d'Aristote*, p. 167.
[98] "Sapientia qua nunc contemplamur Deum non immediate respicit
ipsum Deum, sed effectus quibus ipsum in praesenti contemplamur."
De Virt. In Comm., q. un., a. 12, 11m.
[99] Cf. J. Maritain, *Les degrés du savoir*, p. 457: "La nature divine
demeure voilée, non révélée à notre regard métaphysique, non ob-
jectivée selon ce qu'elle est en elle-même, atteinte dans les choses, in-
touchée en soi. Et pourtant, grâce à l'intellection ananoétique, elle est
constituée l'objet d'une *connaissance absolument solide*, d'une science
contemplant et détaillant en elle des déterminations qui n'impliquent
négation que dans *notre mode de concevoir*."
[100] "Illud est ultimum cognitionis humanae de Deo quod sciat se Deum
nescire in quantum cognoscit, illud quod Deus est, omne ipsum quod de
eo intelligimus, excedere." *De Pot.*, q. 7, a. 5, 14m; "Dicimur in fine
nostrae cognitionis Deum tanquam ignotum cognoscere . . ." *In Boet. De
Trin.*, q. 1, a. 2, 1m. Cf. also: *In I Sent.*, D. 8, q. 1, a. 1, 4m; *De Ver.*,
q. 2, a. 1, 9m; *De Div. Nom.*, c. 7, lect. 4, no. 731; *Cont. Gent.*, I, 30;
III, 39 & 49.
[101] "La grande joie du philosophe est d'avoir l'évidence que Dieu dépasse
toute connaissance, qu'il est, en son absolu, inconnaissable. Le méta-
physicien ne peut se reposer ailleurs; toute autre joie a nécessairement
un objet limité; et cette joie, qui vient du mystère, est déjà à son plan
un avant-goût de la béatitude éternelle . . ." T. Philippe, O.P., "Contemplation métaphysique et mystère de la création," *Revue des sciences
philosophiques et théologiques*, 23 (1934), p. 352.

joy, while deep and genuine, remains rooted in mystery and only serves to increase the longing for more perfect knowledge.

As the mind arrives at the mystery of God, there is born the desire to see God from within, in his essence. The natural wonder—"all men by nature desire to know"[102]—faces its supreme object, the wonderful mystery of infinite being. Curiously enough, while wonder about the subject of metaphysics is stilled,[103] it is really only overshadowed by another wonder, that evoked by the blinding light of being's highest cause.[104] The inherent mystery of existence remains unfathomed, as the mind stands in awe before uncreated being, and human wisdom cries out to see God as he is in himself . . .

---

[102]Aristotle, *Metaphysics*, Bk. I, chap. 1 (980 a 21).

[103]Cf. *In I Meta.*, lect. 3, no. 67: "Erit ergo finis huius scientiae in quem proficere debemus ut causas cognoscentes non admiremur de effectibus."

[104]Two well-known problems are immediately evident in the analysis of metaphysics' incompleteness: that of the natural desire to see God and the question whether or not an affective knowledge of God is possible in the natural order. This latter problem, involving as it does a natural mysticism, suggests in turn the question concerning man's natural love of God. A separate investigation of these problems is beyond our purpose here, being necessarily sacrificed to the attempt at synthesis. However, although solutions to these and other problems could only be sources of light, they do not seem essential to the synthesis as such. And while it may happen in synthetic studies that what is gained in scope may be lost in depth, the author trusts that here as elsewhere in the work the decision to forego an attempt to solve all the problems has been a valid one.

III

THE WISDOM OF
THEOLOGY

The human intellect formed by natural wisdom finds itself at
the threshold of the supernatural. While the metaphysician
is incapable of touching positively the world proper to God,
he does in a sense contact it negatively; at least he knows that
there is much about God of which metaphysics is totally ignorant.[1] Attracted by the mystery confronting him, the natural
wise man could but wish to be enlightened from within that
world closed to his vision. Only if God would make known
what is beyond the reach of nature, could man ever slake his
thirst, however inadequately, for the waters he hears running
within the mountain of the divine. Happily, God has chosen
to do just this. He has revealed himself to man in the Judaeo-
Christian tradition, climaxed in the gift of his Word, the Son of
God, Jesus Christ.

I. FIDES QUAERENS INTELLECTUM—FAITH SEEKING UNDERSTANDING

A. THE ASSENT TO REVELATION

The revelation of the divine mystery made to man by God is
something totally gratuitous. But in the gratuitous offering of
an intellectual object which surpasses man's natural powers,

[1]Cf. the demonstrability of the supernatural order in R. Garrigou-
Lagrange, *De Revelatione* (Rome: Ferrari, 1945) I, 318-30.

something more is required. Unless the human mind be strengthened by a knowing principle higher than its own light, the supernatural object presented in revelation could not call forth man's assent. God, therefore, extends his gracious condescension to embrace, again gratuitously, the gift of grace and the light of faith. In all this there are a number of theological problems open to possible discussion. What is important in the present context—as the transition is made from metaphysical to theological wisdom—is the fact that faith is received in a human intelligence. The nature of this faith which introduces man to God's world is expressed in the following words by the Vatican Council:

> This faith, which is "the beginning of human salvation," the Catholic Church professes to be a supernatural virtue by which under the inspiration and with the aid of God's grace we believe to be true that which he has revealed, not because of intrinsic evidence seen in the natural light of reason but because of the authority of God himself revealing, who can neither deceive nor be deceived.[2]

Faith is a habit of mind, a supernatural virtue of the intellect, whose act is to believe the truths revealed by God. God's revelation of himself invites man's intellectual assent; revelation confronts assent, and in this confrontation two things are especially important for the development which follows here. Revelation, first of all, being offered to the human mind, must be couched in the medium proper to the operations of that mind. This means that divine truths must be proposed to man conceptually, they must be clothed in human concepts.[3] The conceptual medium, however, in which or through which man adheres to revealed truth, does not terminate the act of faith.

[2]"Hanc vero fidem, quae 'humanae salutis initium est,' Ecclesia catholica profitetur, virtutem esse supernaturalem, qua, Dei aspirante et adiuvante gratia, ab eo revelata vera esse credimus, non propter intrinsecam rerum veritatem naturali rationis lumine perspectam, sed propter auctoritatem ipsius Dei revelantis, qui nec falli nec fallere potest." Denz. 1789.

[3]". . . divinae revelationis radius ad nos pervenit secundum modum nostrum. Unde quamvis per revelationem elevemur ad aliquid cognoscendum, quod alias esset nobis ignotum, non tamen ad hoc quod alio modo cognoscamus nisi per sensibilia." *In Boet. De Trin.*, q. 6, a. 3, c.

The intellectual assent reaches beyond the medium to touch the reality contained in concepts: "The act of one who believes does not terminate in the proposition but in the thing."[4] As we shall see later, in discussing the limitations of theology and the corresponding desire to know the mystery of God more immediately, it is this conceptual foundation necessary in faith, which is the source of those limitations.

The other significant point refers not to revelation but to its counterpart, the intellect's assent to the truths proposed. Because revelation does not compel assent—"not because of intrinsic evidence seen in the natural light of reason"[5]—the mind must be moved by the will to accept revealed truth. Deprived of intrinsic evidence, the intellect necessarily remains unimpressed. Man's "yes" to divine truth requires other considerations, which can influence the intellect only by way of the will, for the individual must be convinced that it is good for him to believe, and this requires an affective response to good on the part of the will.[6] Behind this radical affectivity in faith is the prospect of eternal happiness as a promised reward.[7] Faith attracts the individual by making an appeal to his desire for happiness.

Without developing either of these characteristics further here, we shall see later that the conceptual character of revelation

[4]"Actus autem credentis non terminatur ad enuntiabile sed ad rem." *Summa* II-II, q. 1, a. 2, ad 2.

[5]". . . non propter intrinsecam rerum veritatem naturali rationis lumine perspectam." Denz. 1789.

[6]"Actus fidei est credere qui est actus intellectus determinati ad unum ex imperio voluntatis." *In XI Heb.*, lect. 1, no. 553. "Intellectus possibilis determinatur ad hoc quod totaliter adhaereat uni parti; sed hoc est quandoque ab intelligibili, quandoque a voluntate. . . . Quandoque vero intellectus non potest determinari ad alteram partem contradictionis neque statim per ipsas definitiones terminorum, sicut in principiis, nec etiam virtute principiorum, sicut in conclusionibus demonstrativis est; determinatur autem per voluntatem quae elegit assentire uni parti determinate et praecise propter aliquid quod est sufficiens ad movendum voluntatem non autem ad movendum intellectum, utpote quod videtur bonum vel conveniens huic parti assentire." *De Ver.*, q. 14, a. 1, c.

[7]"Movemur ad credendum dictis, inquantum nobis repromittitur, si crediderimus, praemium aeternae vitae . . ." *De Ver.*, q. 14, a. 1, c. On the affective dimension in faith see Labourdette, "La vie théologale selon S. Thomas—affection dans la foi," *Revue thomiste*, 60 (1960) 364-80.

and the affective dimension in the intellect's assent add essential colorings to the nature of theology.

B. FAITH, AN INCHOATIVE WISDOM

Through faith, man possesses a knowledge of God totally un-attainable by natural wisdom. As a valid intellectual grasp of the unique highest cause, faith in some sense might also be considered wisdom, a wisdom of the supernatural order. Strictly speaking, however, faith is but inchoative wisdom; it is a "simple knowledge of the articles which are the principles of all Christian wisdom."[8] As the introduction to the world of super-natural principles, faith remains open to two possible develop-ments which can be traced to the conceptual and affective notes discussed above. As a contemporary theologian remarks:

> The penetration of revealed truth . . . may be realized through supernatural contemplation, based upon an affective union with God; or through theological contemplation, based upon in-tellectual activity which is rational and discursive.[9]

This twofold possibility open to faith becomes the source of two distinct wisdoms, expressed by St. Thomas when he writes:

> Since judgment is proper to the wise man, wisdom is dis-tinguished according to a twofold manner of judging. Someone might judge, first of all, according to inclination . . . secondly, according to knowledge . . . The first manner of judging is proper to that wisdom which is a gift of the Holy Spirit . . . The second is proper to this doctrine (theology), pos-sessed through study, yet whose principles are received through revelation.[10]

[8]". . . cognitio simplex articulorum, quae sunt *principia* totius christianae sapientiae." *In III Sent.*, D. 35, q. 2, a. 1, q1a. 1, 1m. Cf. also *Summa II-II*, q. 19, a. 7, c.

[9]"L'effort de perception de l'objet révélé . . . peut se faire par la voie de la contemplation surnaturelle, sur la base d'une union affective à Dieu; ou bien par la voie de la contemplation théologique, sur la base d'une activité de connaissance de mode rationel et discursif." Y. Congar, O.P., "Théologie," *Dictionnaire de théologie catholique*, T. XV, col. 450.

[10]"Cum iudicium ad sapientem pertinet, secundum duplicem modum iudicandi, dupliciter sapientia accipitur. Contingit enim aliquem iudicare, uno modo per modum inclinationis. . . . Alio modo, per modum cog-nitionis. . . . Primus igitur modus iudicandi de rebus divinis pertinet ad

While faith is a knowledge of highest cause, though it is not cause-conscious, and while its supernatural character makes that knowledge far superior to any merely natural knowledge of God, its full stature as wisdom is incomplete. Conceptually, faith lacks the ordered structure, expressed in terms of principles and conclusions and the myriad dependences and interdependences of various truths, necessary to qualify it as a conceptual wisdom. Moreover, its affectivity is too elemental to establish the complete connaturality required in the more immediate wisdom of the Holy Spirit. On both counts, therefore, faith remains but an inchoative wisdom, open, on the one hand, to conceptual completion through reason, and on the other, to affective deepening through charity. In these two directions are discovered the two wisdoms associated with the supernatural, theology and the gift of wisdom. While they are different wisdoms, neither has any meaning without faith, nor are they totally disparate perfections following upon faith. They find their deepest significance in the common sharing of faith's desire for vision; both are rooted in what is expressed by St. Anselm's phrase: *Fides quaerens intellectum*—faith seeking understanding.[11]

C. FAITH SEEKS UNDERSTANDING

For the moment, our consideration concerns the conceptual penetration of the mysteries of faith—the expansion or further illumination of faith in the affective order will be reserved to

sapientiam quae ponitur donum Spiritus Sancti. . . . Secundus autem modus iudicandi pertinet ad hanc doctrinam, secundum quod per studium habetur, licet eius principia ex revelatione habeantur." *Summa* I, q. 1, a. 6, ad 3. Cf. also II-II, q. 45, a. 2, c.

[11]"Perception réaliste dans une proportion conceptuelle, la foi est lumière divine *dans* une intelligence humaine. Elle est possédée par l'homme, et l'homme pense par elle. Si la foi tend de tout son être à la vision, son appétit lors même qu'il s'efforce à l'intuition, engage normalement l'organisme mental de l'homme: oraison contemplative et spéculation théologique seront des variétés spécifiquement différentes dans leur jeu psychologique; mais en structure théologale, elles ont même objet, même principe, même fin: leur divorce est une infirmité, loin d'être la loi. *Fides quaerens intellectum,* voilà leur commune loi." M. D. Chenu, O.P., "Position de la théologie," *Revue des sciences philosophiques et théologiques,* 24 (1935), p. 253.

the following chapter. Here, what is important is that faith is received in obscurity in a human intelligence, and though the intellect accepts revealed truth with full and certain assent, it finds itself in a state of inquietude. Created for vision, it longs for evidence of the truths affirmed on the strength of the will's influence. This is the basis for St. Augustine's well-known phrase identifying faith: "Cum assensione cogitare."[12] Although the mind assents, reason remains unsatisfied, and its inquiry continues, as it seeks to understand what is revealed in mystery. In that quest theology is born.[13]

As the Christian intelligence seeks to penetrate what it holds by faith, all the resources of rational activity come into play to serve the ideal of *fides quaerens intellectum*. The possibility of a true understanding, even though incomplete, is affirmed by the Vatican Council in the following words:

> When reason, illumined by faith, seeks earnestly, devoutly, and prudently, it does attain with the help of God some under-standing of the mysteries and that a most fruitful one. This is realized through analogy with things known naturally by reason and through the interrelations existing among the mysteries themselves, as well as through the relationship in which these mysteries stand to the final end of man.[14]

In the writings of St. Thomas there are two pertinent texts, which give profound expression to the same Anselmian ideal. The first is taken from his commentary on Boethius's *De Trinitate*: "Similarly, the proximate principle of this science is faith; but its primary source is the divine intellect to which we profess our belief. Faith is in us for this reason, that we

---

[12]*De Praedestinatione Sanctorum*, I, 2. P. L. 44:963. St. Thomas comments on the phrase in *De Ver.*, q. 14, a. 1. Cf. also *Summa* II-II, q. 2, a. 1.

[13]"La théologie est en elle-même un phénomène beaucoup plus simple et primitif (que le statut scientifique), et elle fut créée du jour où les chrétiens, par le mouvement le plus spontané de leur âme religieuse, adoptèrent comme objet de leur pensée et de leur effort d'intelligence les vérités mêmes de leur foi." Deman, "Composantes," p. 420.

[14]"Ac ratio quidem, fide illustrata, cum sedulo, pie et sobrie quaerit, aliquam Deo dante mysteriorum intelligentiam eamque fructuosissimam assequitur, tum ex eorum quae naturaliter cognoscit, analogia, tum e mysteriorum ipsorum nexu inter se et cum fine hominis ultimo." Denz. 1796.

might attain to an understanding of the truths we believe."[15] Here, faith is shown to have no other *raison d'être* than that man might one day understand what has been revealed to him by the divine intellect. Faith is the point of departure, vision will be its term. In the meantime, man seeks, to the extent that he is able, to gain some understanding of what he has received in mystery.

The second text points up more clearly that an enlightened reason is to be the instrument used in the movement toward understanding: "Reason, guided by faith, attains a more adequate grasp of revealed truths and then in a certain manner understands them."[16] Faith alone, implying no more than the mere assent to truth, is incapable of deepening its comprehension of what has been revealed. To make possible that quest for understanding, therefore, it enlists the service of reason. Reason then begins the process, not of solving mysteries, but of penetrating with some degree of understanding that opaque world of the supernatural. Its efforts toward analysis and synthesis, however, together with its discursive movements of induction and deduction, of invention and resolution, are by no means a simple superimposition of philosophy upon faith. While theology uses philosophy, it integrates the light of reason in the higher light of faith. Any other supposition would be monstrous.[17] Just as the Person of the Word assumed a human nature and gave to properly human acts a divine character, so faith raises reason to its level, and what would otherwise be merely natural operations take on a higher perfection as instruments of a higher light. This elevation of reason to the level of faith, permitting reason to concern itself with supernatural truth, is not, as

[15]"Et similiter huius scientiae principium proximum est fides; sed primum est intellectus divinus, cui nos credimus; sed fides est in nobis, ut perveniamus ad intelligendum quae credimus." Q. 2, a. 2, 7m.

[16]"Ratio manuducta per fidem excrescit in hoc ut ipsa credibilia plenius comprehendat, et tunc ipsa quodammodo intelligit." *In I Sent.*, Prol., q. 1, a. 3, sol. 3.

[17]Cf. Maritain, *Les degrés*, p. 500 and *Science et sagesse*, pp. 191-92. See also Congar, "Théologie," col. 454.

some might be inclined to believe, a perversion of faith. As St. Thomas remarks: "Those theologians who use philosophical doctrines in theology by bringing them into the service of faith do not mix water with wine but rather change what is water into wine."[18] Faith welcomes reason, for only through the latter's powers can the conceptual development of the deposit of faith be realized. In the dynamism of *fides quaerens intellectum*, therefore, there is created the science of theology, which St. Augustine characterizes as: "That science through which a healthy faith, leading to true happiness, is given birth, nourished, defended, and strengthened."[19] And the importance of this effort on man's part to penetrate the revealed mystery receives its finest apology in these words of St. Thomas:

> Since the perfection of man consists in union with God, he must strive toward divine things with all that is in him, directing his reason to their investigation, his intellect to their contemplation, according to the text of *Psalm* 72, 28: "It is good for me to adhere to God."[20]

II. The Nature of Theological Wisdom and Its Primary Act

With an understanding of the genesis of theology, expressed in the maxim, *fides quaerens intellectum*, we investigate here the nature of theology and its primary act. An affirmative response to the question, *an sit*, leads quite naturally to the question, *quid sit*—what is theology? Obviously, all the problems which surround an investigation of theology's nature cannot be treated. They are far too vast. The present discussion will

[18]"Unde illi (theologi) qui utuuntur philosophicis documentis in sacra scriptura redigendo in obsequium fidei, non miscent aquam vino, sed convertunt aquam in vinum." *In Boet. De Trin.*, q. 2, a. 3, 5m.

[19]". . . (illa scientia qua) fides saluberrima, quae ad veram beatitudinem ducit, gignitur, nutritur, defenditur, roboratur." *De Trinitate*, L. XIV, c. 1, no. 3. P.L. 42:1037.

[20]"Cum perfectio hominis consistat in coniunctione ad Deum, oportet quod homo ex omnibus quae in ipso sunt quantum potest ad divina innitatur et adducatur, ut intellectus contemplationi et ratio inquisitioni divinorum vacet secundum illud Psal. LXXII, 28: 'Mihi adhaerere Deo bonum est.'" *In Boet. De Trin.*, q. 2, a. 1, c.

be limited to three topics: 1) an examination of theology precisely as wisdom; 2) a determination of its principal or primary act; and 3) a consideration of its transcendent speculative-practical character.

A. THEOLOGY AS WISDOM

As in metaphysics, the first question must concern theology's qualifications as wisdom, crystallized dialectically in the problem, "Is theology science or wisdom?" But before this question can be satisfactorily answered, even properly posed, there are several remarks which must be made.

1. Introductory Remarks

Theology is the child of faith and reason. Supernatural truth, received in faith and developed by reason, is given birth as the divine-human knowledge called theology.[21] Throughout the process, reason uses all the techniques at its command in creating the rational construction of revelation. But these rational techniques are meaningful, only if they serve at the interior of faith's vision.[22] In constructing conceptually its work of theological architecture human intelligence must keep the desired end ever in view, an understanding of the truths of faith. These truths remain forever the primary object of the theologian's attention.

In the activity of order-conscious reason, the truths of faith become the principles of theological thought. Order requires principle, and reason's knowing depends upon order—"It is proper to reason to know order."[23] Further, this characterization

[21]Cf. the ideas of M. J. Scheeben on the genesis of theology in *The Mysteries of Christianity* (transl., C. Vollert, S.J., St. Louis: Herder, 1946), pp. 778-88.

[22]"Selon les discernements à prévoir et avec la discrétion nécessaire, toutes les techniques de la raison seront mises en oeuvre à l'intérieur et au bénéfice de la perception mystique du croyant: morcelage conceptuel, multiplicité des analyses et des jugements, définitions et divisions, comparaisons et classements, inférences, raisonnements en quête d'explication, déduction enfin . . ." Chenu, *Une école de théologie: le Saulchoir* (Etoilles S & O: Le Saulchoir, 1937), p. 70.

[23]". . . proprium (rationis) est cognoscere ordinem." *In I Eth.*, lect. 1, no. 1.

67

of revealed truths as the principles of theology suggests a dual concern of reason: the determination of the various revealed truths as its principles, and its attempt to penetrate those truths with understanding by applying the laws proper to itself. This two-fold effort of reason, embracing at once what is called the *auditus fidei*, on the one hand, and the *intellectus fidei*, on the other, is the basis of the modern distinction between positive and speculative theology.[24] The first concerns whether and how something is revealed and involves a study of scriptural and traditional sources—it is based on authority; the second seeks to disengage the intelligibility of revealed truths in their various relations, interrelations, and implications—it accepts its matter on authority, but is itself based on reason.[25]

Another point requires attention, if only to be mentioned, before the science-wisdom problem can be properly appreciated: the place of history in theology. It is evident that theology must

[24]Cf. the analysis of this duality, which nonetheless does not in any way derogate from theology's essential unity, in Congar, "Théologie," cols. 462-64 & passim. The positive-speculative division of theology finds its most official recognition in the *Schema Constitutionis Dogmaticae De Doctrina Catholica* of the Vatican Council: "Est alia mysteriorum scientia, quae progreditur ex principiis revelatis et ex fide creditis, atque his principiis innititur. Haec intelligentia absit, ut excludatur; ea enim constituitur magna pars sacrae theologiae. Fide nimirum supposita inquiritur quomodo veritates in revelatione sint propositae, quae est theologia *positiva* (ut dici solet); atque inde assumptis etiam veritatibus et principiis rationalibus aliqua analogica intelligentia rerum per revelationem cognitarum deducitur, quid sint in seipsis: 'fides quaerens intellectum'; haec est theologia *speculativa.*" Mansi, *Amplissima Collectio Conciliorum*, T. 50, col. 84.

[25]Cf. the distinction made by St. Thomas between the question, *an sit verum*, and the question, *quomodo sit verum*, in theological discussion and the corresponding roles played by authority and reason (*Quodl. IV, q. 9, a. 3, c.*). The movement from assent to understanding involves the whole of theology according to diverse lines of reflection. Positive theology includes: "Investigation critique du donné pour déterminer ce qui est vraiment révélé ou jusqu'à quel point un énoncé bénéficie de l'-autorité de la révélation *(an sit revelatum);* réflection historique sur la présentation de la révélation et son développement concret *(quomodo revelatum est).*" Speculative theology represents "réflexion spéculative en vue de dégager l'intelligibilité propre des vérités révélées dans leurs connexions et leurs implications et d'en constituer la synthèse scientifique *(quid sit quod revelatum est).*" M. Labourdette, O.P., "La théologie science de la foi," *Revue thomiste*, 46 (1946), p. 24.

be interested in history, for its object involves the plan of salvation and that plan is bound to time in its revelation and realization.[26] Certainly, positive theology, though formally theology and not history, must be significantly concerned with history in the examination of sources. But the realism with which history enriches theology is not limited to the past. The "mystery hidden for ages and generations"[27] and revealed in Christ is being realized, made real, continuously in time, and the theologian can never cut himself or his doctrine off from that fact. Although distinction can truly be made, and perhaps it is not made often enough, between the doctrinal and the historical in theology, the objective must always be *distinguer pour unir*. Theology is the science of salvation and salvation is realized in history.

With these preliminary remarks made to shelve the separate problems of history and the speculative-positive relationship in theology, we can approach the problem basic to our theme: Whether theology is purely science or wisdom.

2. The Statement of the Problem

Historically, the problem of theology as science or wisdom finds its roots in the thirteenth century. At that time the introduction of the Aristotelian corpus and its strict notion of science prompted the question of theology's qualifications as science. This was immediately recognized as demanding an option between the traditional Augustinian concept of wisdom and Aristotle's concept of science. "Is theology an affective knowledge or a scientific demonstration?" is the way the question was posed.[28] While the theologians of the first half of the century opted for the Augustinian notion of wisdom, St. Thomas was among the

---

[26]Cf. the remarks found in Chenu, "Position," p. 246 & passim.
[27]*Col.* 1:26.
[28]"La théologie est-elle une connaissance savoureuse ou une démonstration scientifique?" J. Leclercq, O.S.B., "La théologie comme science d'après la littérature quodlibétique," *Recherches de théologie ancienne et médiévale*, 11 (1939), p. 273.

first to demonstrate that theology is science.[29] Accepting from Aristotle the notion of subalternation, he was able to show that a theologian, although believing his principles, could still fulfill the demands of scientific discourse: ". . . from things known one attains the knowledge of things unknown."[30] However, St. Thomas did not merely justify theology's character as science; he qualified that identification profoundly when he added that theology is wisdom.[31] The significance of this shall be seen below.

In the theological tradition following St. Thomas perhaps too much emphasis has been placed upon the notion of theology as science.[32] Because science is of conclusions, the impression may be given that the theologian is not really interested in the truths of faith, but rather in the conclusions. Revealed truths are merely principles and viewed literally as points of departure, not as objects of the intellect's primary concern. For the moment, this must be left without comment, for we are interested here in the statement of the problem that has developed in modern controversy.

The idea has developed that theology as science suggests nothing more than what has been called, aptly or inaptly, "conclusion-theology," and, as a result, severe criticisms have been levelled against it. One of the more popular of these criticisms is to be found in the writings of a German writer,

[29]"Duplex est scientiarum genus. Quaedam enim sunt, quae procedunt ex principiis notis lumine naturali intellectus, sicut arithmetica, geometria, et huiusmodi. Quaedam vero sunt, quae procedunt ex principiis notis lumine superioris scientiae: sicut perspectiva procedit ex principiis notificatis per geometriam, et musica ex principiis per arithmeticam notis. Et hoc modo sacra doctrina est scientia: quia procedit ex principiis notis lumine superioris scientiae, quae scilicet est scientia Dei et beatorum. Unde sicut musica credit principia tradita sibi ab arithmetico, ita doctrina sacra credit principia revelata sibi a Deo." *Summa* I, q. 1, a. 2, c. Cf. also *In I Sent.*, Prol., q. 1, a. 3, q1a. 2; *In Boet. De Trin.*, q. 2, a. 2.

[30]". . . ex aliquibus notis alia ignotiora cognoscantur." *In Boet. De Trin.*, q. 2, a. 2, c. On the notion of subalternation, cf. Chenu, *La théologie comme science au XIIIe siècle* (3e édition, Paris: Vrin, 1957), pp. 80-85.

[31]Cf. *Summa* I, q. 1, a. 6; *In I Sent.*, Prol., q. 1, a. 3, q1a. 3.

[32]Cf. Congar, "Théologie," col. 459.

Johannes Beumer, S.J.[33] In his *Theologie als Glaubensverständnis* the author traces historically the notion, *intellectus fidei*, from the Fathers, through the scholastic period and the mystics, to the Vatican Council's statement on the nature of theology.[34] In the process Fr. Beumer sees St. Thomas as unfaithful to the Augustinian-Anselmian *fides quaerens intellectum*. Admitting that in his earlier works[35] St. Thomas views theology in this light, he claims that in the *Summa theologiae* all this is forgotten in favor of an articulated presentation of Aristotle's concept of subalternated science. This necessitates a departure from an *intellectus fidei*.[36] Theology is no longer concerned with the revealed truths, except as mere points of departure—"über die Glaubensartikel hinaus"[37]—with this qualification, that they hold the theologian's attention for their defense.[38]

This portrait of St. Thomas's theology, as having no real interest in the revealed truths themselves, leads Fr. Beumer

---

[33]The most significant of his works which concern directly St. Thomas's conception of theology are: "Conclusionstheologie?" *Zeitschrift für katholische Theologie*, 63 (1939) 360-65; *Theologie als Glaubensverständnis* (Würzburg: Echter, 1953); "Thomas von Aquin zum Wesen der Theologie," *Scholastik*, 30 (1955) 195-214.

[34]Denz. 1796.

[35]*In I Sent.*, Prol., q. 1, a. 3, sol. 3; *In Boet. De Trin.*, q. 2, a. 2, 7m. Cf. also *Theologie als Glaubensverständnis*, pp. 82-83.

[36]"Nun benutzt aber der Aquinate in seiner 'Summa Theologica,' wie längst erwiesen ist und von niemand bestritten wird, den aristotelischen Wissenschaftsbegriff in seiner ganzen Strenge für die Theologie. Danach ist aber 'Wissenschaft' (*scientia* in der Sprache der Schule) einzuschränken auf das Wissen um die Schlussfolgerungen, während für die Prinzipien nur Einsicht (*intellectus*) in Frage kommt. In der Anwendung auf die Theologie musste das ergeben, dass deren nicht-einsichtige Prinzipien, die Glaubensartikel, durch die *subalternatio* unter das Wissen Gottes und der Seligen des Himmels zu Prinzipien wurden, die nur im Glauben erfasst werden können, und dass die Wissenschaft des Glaubens nichts anderes als die Schlussfolgerungen zugewiesen bekam. Thomas konnte also gut von einer *scientia fidei* reden, musste aber dabei die Einschränkung auf die *conclusiones* mitmachen, damit der aristotelische Begriff gewahrt blieb. Er konnte aber nicht mehr an einem *intellectus fidei* festhalten . . ." *Theologie als Glaubensverständnis*, pp. 90-91.

[37]"Thomas von Aquin zum Wesen," p. 213.

[38]". . . die Aufgabe der Glaubenswissenschaft gegenüber den Offensbarungswahrheiten wird in die Verteidigung und in den Nachweis der Widerspruchslosigkeit verlegt." *Theologie als Glaubensverständnis*, pp. 91-92.

to deny St. Thomas a place in the positive evolutionary tradition stemming from St. Augustine to the Vatican Council. With the accent placed upon Aristotelian science, the depth and richness of the Augustinian *intellectus fidei* was lost in the *Summa theologiae,* and the Council's re-emphasis must mean, therefore, a return to the notion of theology before St. Thomas. To say the least, such a position is open to question. In the paragraphs that follow an attempt will be made to show that, whatever may be said for the alleged extremes of later Thomism, St. Thomas himself escapes the devastating indictment claimed valid by Fr. Beumer.

3. The Solution to the Problem

The defense of St. Thomas's conception of theology will rest upon two fundamental points. First, the movement from the idea of science to the implications of the modern phrase, "conclusion-theology," is rooted in a misconception of the nature of science; and second, when St. Thomas bestows the name, *wisdom,* on theology, he implies far more than simply that "Sacred doctrine treats of God inasmuch as he is highest cause."[39]

a. The Nature of Science

When discussing the difference between wisdom's demonstrative function and its primary act of contemplation in the preceding chapter, it was pointed out that all demonstration, the act proper to science, demands resolution, the return to principles. A conclusion of science is viewed in the light of its principles.

---

[39]"Der 6. Artikel *(Utrum haec doctrina sit sapientia)* könnte noch am ehesten Anlass bieten, die positive Aufgabe der Theologie gegenüber den Glaubenswahrheiten herauszustellen, aber heisst dort nur: *Sacra autem doctrina determinat de Deo secundum quod est altissima causa* und in der Antwort auf obj. 1. wird nur neuerdings die *scientia subalternata* betont: *Sacra doctrina non supponit sua principia ab aliqua scientia humana, sed a scientia divina, a qua, sicut a summa sapientia, omnis nostra cognitio ordinatur." Theologie als Glaubensverständnis,* p. 85, note 16. Two things may be noted here in passing: first, that the concept of wisdom involves more than a determination of highest cause, though this is the basis for its richness of implication; second, that the response here cited merely answers an obvious objection to theology's qualifications as wisdom; the restatement of subalternation is not a denial of wisdom's possibilities regarding the truths of faith.

This indicates that an identification of scientific reasoning as a departure, in the literal sense, from the principles is somewhat simplist. It is true that in formulating the nature of the rational discursus as a "proceeding *from* or *out of* principles"[40] and in emphasizing science as concerned with conclusions[41] the necessary appreciation of the place of principles in science may be obscured. But if the act of demonstration is examined in its fullness, if the essential relationship between *ratio* and *intellectus* is understood[42], then science will be truly evaluated and valued as "moving from principles to conclusions in order to grasp both principles and conclusions in a single view, a process toward a terminal understanding."[43] The notion of science, suggesting a movement to conclusions which become objects of the intellect's attention independent of their principles, is without foundation. Conclusions are valid only as viewed in their principles. St. Thomas writes:

> The investigation of reason proceeds from simple intuitive understanding—out of the principles held by understanding one proceeds to investigation—and it is terminated in the certitude of understanding, as the conclusions reached are resolved into the principles wherein their certitude is based.[44]

---

[40]*In I Post. Anal.*, lect. 4, no. 11; *In Boet. de Trin.*, q. 2, a. 2, c; *Summa* I, q. 1, a. 2, c.

[41]*In I Sent.*, Prol., q. 1, a. 3, sol. 3; *In I Post. Anal.*, lect. 7, no. 6.

[42]Cf. the study made of these notions by J. Peghaire, *Intellectus et ratio selon St. Thomas d'Aquin* (Paris: Vrin, 1936).

[43]B. Lonergan, S.J., "Theology and Understanding," *Gregorianum*, 35 (1954), pp. 634-35.

[44]"Inquisitio autem rationis sicut a simplici intuitu intellectus progreditur, quia ex principiis quae quis intellectu tenet ad inquisitionem procedit, ita etiam ad intellectus certitudinem terminatur, dum conclusiones inventae in principia resolvuntur in quibus certitudinem habent." *In III Sent.*, D. 35, q. 1, a. 2, sol. 2. In a similar context we find: "Ultimus enim terminus ad quem rationis inquisitio perducere debet, est intellectus principiorum, in quae resolvendo iudicamus; quod quidem quando fit non dicitur processus vel probatio rationabilis, sed demonstratio." *In Boet. De Trin.*, q. 6, a. 1, c. (ad primam quaestionem); and "Rationalis consideratio ad intellectualem terminatur secundum viam resolutionis, inquantum ratio ex multis colligit unam et simplicem veritatem. Et rursum, intellectualis consideratio est principium rationalis secundum viam compositionis vel inventionis, inquantum intellectus in uno multitudinem comprehendit. Illa consideratio, quae est terminus totius humanae ratiocinationis, maxime est intellectualis consideratio." *Ibid.*, (ad tertiam quaestionem).

The "proceeding from principles" becomes meaningful only in the return—the "going-out" looks only to the "coming-back." In applying this particular instance of the Platonic idea of *exitus-reditus* to theology, it becomes evident that the scientific nature of theology does not preclude an interest in the truths of faith. The pejorative sense in which the phrase, "conclusion-theology," is used cannot be substantiated in the adequate picture of theological epistemology.

While the position of St. Thomas on theology as science would be unfairly distorted if he were accused of lacking interest in revealed truths themselves, the presentation of his position to the modern world, to judge from Fr. Beumer's criticisms, has failed to defend that interest. It seems true, however, that that failure is not entirely due to the inadequate notion of science referred to above. Even more responsible is the exclusive identification of theology with science, for although science does involve initial and terminal interest in principles, its proper object is the conclusion. The tradition following upon St. Thomas, in its preoccupation with justifying theology as a science with non-evident principles, apparently lost sight of its perfection as wisdom.[45] Attention was drawn away from principles to be focused too exclusively on the conclusion[46], and this mistaken

For other texts, see the references given above in chapter two, note 79. Cf. also the article of S. E. Dolan, F.S.C., "Resolution and Composition in Speculative and Practical Discourse," in *Laval théologique et philosophique*, 6 (1950) 9-62.

[45]"Il concetto di scienza, applicato alla teologia, è un concetto analogico che esige un'applicazione suo modo, e va corretto e completato con l'altro concetto di sapienza che conviene alla teologia non meno che il concetto di scienza." M. Daffara, "La teologia come scienza nella Somma teologica di S. Tommaso," *Sapienza*, 1 (1948), p. 15.

[46]As mentioned above, Congar suggests this exclusiveness. He tempers the criticism, however, by saying that although "commentator" Thomism has emphasized the Aristotelian notion of science, "elle ne présente pas la ligne exclusive de leur pensée sur la nature de la théologie. A lire Bañez (révélation virtuelle) et Jean de S. Thomas (raison comme purement instrumentale), en particulier, il nous semble que leur position en cette matière est caractérisée surtout par un effort pour marquer combien la théologie se construit à l'intérieur de la foi." *Bulletin thomiste*, 5 (1937-39), p. 493, note 1. Cf. also S. Breton, "Logique et théologie," *Revue des sciences philosophiques et théologiques*, 44 (1960), p. 420, note 6.

epistemological emphasis invited the incisive criticism now being levelled against theological science.

One of the reasons for this preoccupation with the conclusion, perhaps, is the identification of theology's objective light, its *objectum formale quo* in the language of the school, as virtual revelation.[47] Although this determination of theology's light is open to broader interpretation, traditionally it has been too often identified with the purely deductive process, and, therefore, limits theology to interest in the strict conclusion.[48] The notion of virtual revelation seems valid only if purified of its exclusively deductive connotations, for the understanding of revealed truths themselves in their relations and interrelations of order and analogy, of exemplarity, efficiency, and finality does not depend *uniquely* upon discursive reasoning.[49] The objective light would then correspond adequately to its sub-

---

[47]Apparently attributable to Bañez, according to Congar, who writes sympathetically by saying: "(lumen sub quo) C'est la Révélation surnaturelle reçue dans la foi en tant que s'exprimant et se développant dans une vie intellectuelle humaine de forme rationelle et scientifique: *Revelatio virtualis,* disent les commentateurs de St. Thomas depuis Bañez . . . la lumière de la foi en tant qu'elle se conjoint celle de la raison, l'informe, la dirige et se sert d'elle pour constituer son objet en un corps de doctrines de forme rationelle et scientifique." in "Théologie," cols. 451-52. Whether or not the notion of virtual revelation in its generally accepted interpretation, is broad enough to receive such a favorable commentary is problematic.

[48]Cf. the criticism made of virtual revelation's insufficiency by Muniz, "De diversis muneribus," pp. 106-10. While important in pointing up the problem, this criticism does not seem entirely convincing, for virtual revelation can be interpreted in a way that does not derogate from theology's interest in revelation itself. The immediacy of virtual revelation's concern for revealed truth seems to depend largely upon the sense given to the word, conclusion. If conclusion is limited to signify the so-called theological conclusion (one inferred from two premises, one of which is purely rational), that immediacy, though not exactly compromised, becomes less evident. However, if the word is not restricted to mean only the "theological conclusion," but is given its full significance as denoting simply the result of all theological reasoning, virtual revelation becomes more respectable. When reasoning in theology concerns two revealed premises, the light of virtual revelation, far from being out of touch with revelation, illuminates the revealed truths themselves.

[49]All that theology does regarding the revealed principles themselves does not involve precisely a movement of science. Cf. John of St. Thomas, *Curs. Theol.,* In I-II, qq. 68-70, Disp. 18, a. 4, nos. 46-48 (Laval, nos. 686-93).

A theology of wisdom

jective counterpart, expressed in the phraseology of St. Thomas as *ratio manuducta per fidem*,[50]—reason guided by faith—and by the Vatican Council as *ratio fide illustrata*[51]—reason illumined by faith. To restrict the light of theology to demonstrative discourse is to confuse the part for the whole. Reason, illumined and led by faith, is interested in every possible avenue of intelligibility which can ultimately realize the understanding sought by faith. That means that the principles themselves, even without reference to possible conclusions, demand her attention. Assigning to theology, without any qualification, the

[50]*In I Sent.*, Prol., q. 1, a. 3, sol. 3. In the *Summa Theologiae* St. Thomas characterizes the objective light of theology by the phrase, "divinitus revelabilia"—things are viewed in theology in the light of their revelability (Cf. *Summa* I, q. 1, a. 3, c. & ad 2). But what is meant precisely by this terminology? First of all, theology seeks ultimately to disengage whatever intelligibility is open to human intelligence in revealed truth. Everything it considers is related to revelation, either as having been actually revealed or as serving toward understanding what has been revealed. Nothing else occupies the attention of reason illumined by faith. The common denominator of this two-fold consideration is not what is *revelatum*, but rather, what is *revelabile*, i.e., that which shares an immediate reference to revelation and its rational intelligibility, and, therefore, could be an object of revelation itself. The clarification added by St. Thomas, "divino lumine cognoscibilia" (*Summa* I, q. 1, a. 4, c.), seems to require a similar interpretation. All knowledge which without faith would lack either validity or significance comes within the competence of theology.

[51]Denz. 1796. There is a problem which remains in determining the exact nature of theology's subjective light, "ratio manuducta per fidem." Does faith enter to change intrinsically reason's natural light, or is it rather a material-formal combination with faith presenting the truths and reason working according to its natural processes? The latter supposition, based upon the distinction between material and formal logic, seems more intelligible, for it is difficult to see how reason's natural light could be changed intrinsically. In the union of faith and reason, therefore, there is a new light, but in this sense, that the material truth of theology, the necessity of its propositions, is for the most part from faith (reason provides some of the matter in the case of the theological conclusion), its formal truth, from reason. Fr. W. A. Wallace, citing John of St. Thomas (*Curs. Theol.* In I, 1, disp. 2, a. 7), expresses it this way: "The illation or reasoning process by which the theological conclusion is deduced is itself a human one, and thus is formally natural, although it is radically and originatively supernatural under the influx of the premise of faith. And despite the fact that reason and faith concur in the understanding of the premises, there is only one light under which the conclusion is seen: the participated *lumen divinum* of sacred theology." *The Role of Demonstration in Moral Theology* (Washington: Thomist Press, 1962), pp. 43-44.

76

virtually revealed or even *that which can be revealed* as its object, when faith views but *what has been actually revealed,* —this "runs the risk of not pointing up the effective interiority of the theologian's rational effort within revealed truth, and this has sometimes reflected theology as being outside faith."[52]

b. The Implications of Wisdom

Whatever may be conjectured as the reason or reasons why theology is seen by some to have lost sight of faith, there seems to exist a tendency in the Thomistic tradition to overlook the truth that for St. Thomas theology is not only science, it is above all, wisdom. A defense of the full stature of science is not enough to dispel the illusion that the attention of theology remains unengaged by revealed truths themselves. The highest dignity of theology is that it is wisdom, and re-emphasis upon this fact should do much to allay the fears of a mere "conclusion-theology."

In the preceding chapter we saw that, while science is interested in principles only insofar as they are related to its conclusions, wisdom not only considers conclusions in the light of principles, it also judges the principles themselves, evaluating and defending their content.[53] It should be evident, therefore, that theology's concern for revealed truths themselves is fully vali-

---

[52]"(cette distinction) court le risque de ne pas ménager l'intériorité effective du travail rationel du théologien *dans* le donné révélé, et elle a parfois reflété un certain extrinsécisme de la théologie par rapport à la foi." Chenu, *Théologie comme science,* pp. 83-84. This risk seems to have been run by Fr. Chenu himself in 1927, when he wrote that for St. Thomas, "L'Ecriture, l'article de foi est non plus la matière même, le sujet de l'exposé et de la recherche, comme dans la *sacra doctrina* du XIIe siècle, mais le *principe, préalablement* connu à partir duquel on travaille selon toutes les exigences et les lois de la *demonstratio* aristotélicienne. Tel est le sens profond de la première question de la Somme." *Archives d'histoire doctrinale et littéraire du moyen age,* 2 (1927), p. 33. Fr. A. Hayen also notices a more ample (and presumably more acceptable) treatment of theological deduction in the third edition of *Théologie comme science.* Cf. "La théologie aux XIIe, XIIIe et XXe siècles," *Nouvelle revue théologique,* 79 (1957), p. 1028.

[53]Cf. *Summa* I-II, q. 66, a. 5, ad 4; *In I Sent.,* Prol., q. 1, a. 3, sol. 1: "Sed sapientia . . . considerat conclusiones et principia; et ideo sapientia est scientia et intellectus; cum scientia sit de conclusionibus et intellectus de principiis."

dated the moment it is understood to be truly wisdom. But does St. Thomas actually think of it as wisdom?

In the *Summa theologiae* we find:

> He therefore who considers absolutely the highest cause of the whole universe, which is God, is called supremely wise . . . Sacred doctrine, however, most properly treats of God as he is highest cause, because it considers him not only with respect to that which is knowable through creatures but also in the light of that which God knows concerning himself and which he communicated to others by revelation. Sacred doctrine, therefore, is most properly called wisdom.[54]

With this should be noted, also, the insistence of St. Thomas upon God as the proper subject of theology; other things are considered only insofar as they have God for their principle and end.[55] With God as the center of theological investigation and creatures viewed only in the light of their relation to him as highest exemplary, efficient, and final cause, theology's claim to being a true wisdom is conclusive, and one can only wonder why so much has been said or written on theology exclusively as science. As Cajetan so justly remarks: "It seems foolish to ask whether the whole of theology, embracing within itself both principles and conclusions, is science, since it is evident that there is no science of principles."[56] If St. Thomas's notion of theology as wisdom had been adequately presented, the criticisms, such as those of Fr. Beumer, perhaps would never have been made.

[54]"Ille igitur qui considerat simpliciter altissimam causam totius universi, quae Deus est, maxime sapiens dicitur. . . . Sacra autem doctrina propriissime determinat de Deo secundum quod est altissima causa, quia non solum quantum ad illud quod est per creaturas cognoscibile; sed etiam quantum ad id quod notum est sibi soli de seipso, et aliis per revelationem communicatum. Unde sacra doctrina maxime dicitur sapientia." *Summa* I, q. 1, a. 6, c. Cf. also *In I Sent.*, Prol., q. 1, a. 3, sol. 1 & 3; *In II Sent.*, Prol., in initio.
[55]*Summa* I, q. 1, a. 7, c. Cf. also *In Boet. De Trin.*, q. 5, a. 4, c. & 8m. The precisions given here and in the *Summa* seem to be a further development of doctrine beyond the position expressed in *In I Sent.*, Prol., q. 1, a. 4, sol. & 1m. See Cajetan, *Commentaria in Summam Theologiae*, I, q. 1, a. 7; also Gagnebet, "Dieu sujet de la théologie selon Saint Thomas d'Aquin," *Analecta gregoriana*, 68 (1954) 41-55.
[56]*Commentaria in Summam Theologiae*, I, q. 1, a. 2, no. 1.

Theology, however, is not wisdom in precisely the same way as is metaphysics. It is a more perfect wisdom, for it begins with the highest cause, while metaphysics terminates there. In the words of St. Bonaventure: "For this alone (theology) is a perfect wisdom, beginning as it does from the highest cause, the principle of everything caused, which is where the considerations of philosophy terminate."[57] This finds an echo in St. Thomas, who compares theology to metaphysics by saying:

> We affirm that theology is a wisdom because it considers highest causes and that it is supreme among all the sciences, privileged to order all the others. It must also be called more a wisdom than metaphysics because it considers highest causes according to the mode of the causes themselves, in the light of revelation immediately received from God, while metaphysics treats of highest causes in the light of reasons taken from creatures.[58]

Theology, moving from God to creatures, reverses the order found in purely natural wisdom, which ascends from creatures to their highest cause in God.[59] But this superiority of theology as wisdom to metaphysics as wisdom is changed if the comparison

---

[57]"Ipsa (theologia) enim sola est sapientia perfecta, quae incipit a causa summa, ut est principium causatorum, ubi terminatur cognitio philosophica." *Breviloquium*, Pars I, c. 1 (cited by Grabmann, *Die theologische Erkenntnis- und Einleitungslehre des heiligen Thomas von Aquin* [Thomistische Studien, Band IV—Freiburg in S.: Paulusverlag, 1948], p. 199).

[58]"Dicimus quod est sapientia eo quod altissimas causas considerat et est sicut caput et principalis et ordinatrix omnium scientiarum; et est etiam magis dicenda sapientia quam metaphysica, quia altissimas causas considerat per modum ipsarum causarum, quia per inspirationem a Deo immediate acceptam; metaphysica autem considerat altissimas causas per rationes ex creaturis assumptas." *In I Sent.*, Prol., q. 1, a. 3, sol. 1. This suggests the inverse order followed by the metaphysician and the theologian, respectively, pointed up in *Cont. Gent.*, II, 4: "Non eodem ordine utraque doctrina procedit. Nam in doctrina philosophiae, quae creaturas secundum se considerat et ex eis in Dei cognitionem perducit, prima est consideratio de creaturis et ultima de Deo. In doctrina vero fidei, quae creaturas non nisi in ordine ad Deum considerat, primo est consideratio Dei et postmodum creaturarum. Et sic est perfectior: utpote Dei cognitioni similior, qui seipsum cognoscens alia intuetur." Cf. also *In II Sent.*, Prol., in init.

[59]Cf. the analysis of the difference between philosophy and theology found in J. Lenz, "Thomistische Philosophie als Lebensweisheit," p. 331.

is made at the level of wisdom's demonstrative function. Here metaphysics is more perfect in virtue of reasoning from evident principles, which the inevidence of faith denies to theology.

If theology is a true realization of acquired wisdom, it must be, like metaphysics, a potential whole, embracing a number of diverse functions.[60] Its most perfect act, its primary act, is contemplation, but it also includes the interpretation and defense of its principles, the demonstrative process of strict science, as well as the judgment and negative control of the lower sciences. Because theology is radically supernatural, these functions will be different from their metaphysical counterparts, as shall be shown later.

While theology's similarity to metaphysics is important, it does not suggest, as does a modern theologian: ". . . in a word, it might be said that theology is a metaphysics of revelation or a metaphysics of faith."[61] The integration of reason and faith precludes the rationalism suggested in such a position. Not a mere superimposition of philosophy upon faith, the structure of theological wisdom remains on a higher level, grounded in the supernatural, with God, the unique highest cause, as its subject, and reason as the instrument of an illuminating faith for its light.

Without undue emphasis on theology's vital concern for its principles, which here would be a bit premature, it should nonetheless be evident that the breadth connoted by the concept of wisdom should help to dispel the illusion of a so-called conclusion-theology. The richness of these connotations should become apparent in the pages that follow. In those pages theological

[60]Cf. the article already cited of F. Muniz, "De diversis muneribus," pp. 93-123. The author's definition of theology emphasizes its sapiential character and suggests adequately its concern for revealed truths themselves: "Sapientia discursiva sub lumine divinae revelationis circa omnem veritatem sive immediate et formaliter sive mediate et virtualiter a Deo revelatam." p. 113.

[61]". . . uno verbo posset dici quod Theologia est Metaphysica Revelationis seu Metaphysica Fidei." Muniz, *Ibid.*, p. 114.

contemplation, as the primary act of a divine-human wisdom, will be discussed, together with the implications of theology's speculative-practical character and the other sapiential acts proper to it.

B. THEOLOGY'S PRIMARY ACT: CONTEMPLATION

When St. Thomas discusses the purpose of theology or sacred doctrine, he writes: "The ultimate end of this doctrine is the contemplation of Truth itself in heaven."[62] Without confronting here the problem of sacred doctrine's precise meaning[63], it can be seen from what follows in the text cited that theology, and not faith alone, is in question. If theology's end, therefore, its ultimate *raison d'être,* is the act of contemplation to be realized in heaven, its perfection here on earth must be the greatest approximation to that end. Contemplation is of the essence of theology, not only because theology is a wisdom, but also because faith engages man supernaturally and orders him to the contemplative happiness of heaven.

It has been said that faith does not contemplate, it adheres.[64] This distinction implies that faith, as a pure assent, is contemplatively incomplete, open to the wisdoms mentioned earlier, one, a rational construction of revealed truth, the other, a quasi-

[62]*In I Sent.,* Prol., q. 1, a. 3, sol. 1.

[63]It should be said in passing, however, that the traditional problem finds a somewhat questionable solution in one of the recent works to appear on the subject: G. Van Ackeren, S.J., *Sacra Doctrina: The Subject of the First Question of the Summa Theologica of St. Thomas Aquinas* (Rome: Catholic Book Agency, 1952). The identification of *sacra doctrina* in all its uses as "the generation of knowledge (of salvation), an operation induced in the intellect of the disciple terminating in new knowledge acquired" (p. 118) seems to forget the distinction between speculative and practical. Here *doctrina* is but an art and therefore only practical, and the divine-human wisdom in question is reduced to teaching. What is taught and what is learned may be wisdom; the teaching itself can never be.

[64]"La foi ne contemple pas, elle adhère." M. Philipon, O.P., "La théologie comme science suprème de la vie humaine," *Revue thomiste,* 18 (1935), p. 397. This seems to belie the remark made by another theologian, who writes: "C'est la contemplation qui suscite une théologie, non la théologie qui conduirait à la contemplation." Chenu, *Une école,* p. 54.

experimental knowledge of the reality attained in faith. The first of these wisdoms, the concern of the present chapter, is one of the two acquired habits of contemplation, distinguished first by St. Thomas.[65] As acquired, it has much in common with its philosophical counterpart, metaphysics, which permits the contemplative act of theology to be discussed according to the same order of topics followed in treating metaphysical contemplation: 1) contemplation in its relation to God; 2) the implications of end and happiness; 3) the note of affectivity involved; and 4) the realism of theological contemplation.

1. Theological Contemplation and God

We have seen that contemplation suggests a *simplex intuitus veritatis* and that, in its fullest sense, it connotes more than truth held as a mere object of knowledge. If metaphysical contemplation becomes meaningful in its attainment of God as highest cause and its ordered view of creation in relation to that cause, how much truer this is of theology. Theology does not rise from the limited, finite wrappings of created being to contemplate the cause of that being; it enjoys contact with God from the very beginning, a contact not with the architectural master of the natural order, but with him to whom, as children destined for glory, we cry, "Abba, Father!"[66] The supernatural world into which faith introduces man presents God as he is in himself, not as mirrored in his creatures, and theology, as a "certain impression of the divine knowledge,"[67] reflects this higher perfection. Just as God sees himself and others in himself, so theology participates that view by contemplating God and all things as they are related to God.

"All things have God for their principle and their end, all things are meaningful in relation to God. It belongs to theological contemplation to reconstruct and relive in the intellectual order

[65]Cf. P. Philippe, O.P., "La contemplation au XIIIe siècle," *Dictionnaire de spiritualité*, T. II, col. 1984.

[66]*Rom.* 8:15.

[67]". . . quaedam impressio divinae scientiae." *Summa* I, q. 1, a. 3, ad 2.

that theocentric synthesis of reality."[68] Wisdom's order is realized here above the highest reaches of metaphysics, in the ordering of reality as referred to the supernatural. This is the contemplation of the theologian, the fruit of the rational construction of revealed truth, and it characterizes the primary act of the supreme acquired wisdom.[69] The *videre omnia in conspectu Dei* becomes a view made more profound by the added depth of the supernatural dimension.

Since wisdom implies essentially a contact with God, each wisdom must be judged by the nature of that contact. The contact of theology, rooted in faith, is obviously superior to that of metaphysics, which cannot touch, even obscurely, the intimacy of the Trinity. Based upon faith in its human imitation or reproduction of God's own knowledge, theology imports all the implications of the supernatural order, and above all, God as the ultimate supernatural end of man. This implication of finality gives to the subordinated hierarchical perspective, in which the theologian views God and his creation, its fullest significance. The connections seen to exist among the revealed mysteries themselves, contemplated in their reference to God, introduce a contemplation of those same truths in their relation to man's end.[70]

2. Theological Contemplation and Finality

Order in wisdom's contemplation, as we saw in the texts examined earlier, finds its ultimate source in the idea of end: "It is the wise man who orders, for the ordering of things is possible

[68]"Toutes choses ont Dieu pour principe et pour fin, toutes choses s'expliquent par rapport à Dieu. Cette synthèse théocentrique dans l'ordre des réalités, il appartient à la contemplation théologique de la reconstruire et de la revivre dans l'ordre de la connaissance." Congar, *Bulletin thomiste,* 5 (1937-39), p. 495.

[69]"Le principe de cette ordonnance, c'est la Déité elle-même, obscurément connue, telle qu'elle s'est manifestée à nous. C'est pourquoi la théologie est la sagesse suprème, parce qu'elle explique tout à la lumière de Dieu. Elle le manifeste à nous tel qu'il se connaît lui-même et elle nous manifeste en lui les créatures telles qu'il les voit dans le regard qu'il porte sur lui-même: 'velut quaedam impressio divinae scientiae.'" Gagnebet, "La nature," p. 239.

[70]Cf. Denz. 1796.

only with a knowledge of things in their mutual interrelations as well as in reference to something above and beyond them—their end."[71] Without end, there can be no order, there can be no reality, at least no caused reality; *finis est causa causarum.*[72] Without the notion and the reality of end or final cause, all possibility of contemplation is denied. But God is identified with end, and he is viewed by theology precisely as man's ultimate supernatural end to be attained fully in the beatific vision. This is the basis for theological wisdom's contemplative realization of the maxim, *sapientis est ordinare.*

With God as theology's subject, there is immediate "reference to a double object: God as author of happiness and the divine plan of the means to attain that happiness, that is to say, to the two-fold mystery of God: the necessary mystery of his Trinitarian life and the free mystery of our salvation through the redemptive Incarnation."[73] God as he communicates himself to men, as he is their last end, is the reason for revelation[74], and theology as it emanates from that revelation must likewise look to God as man's last end and happiness. "If sacred science were to develop in another direction, it would soon no longer be the science of salvation and sanctification."[75] In the light of this, how untrue it is to think of theology as a mere application of philosophy to faith; theology is truly a religious science with an object involving man's destiny.[76]

[71]"Ordinare sapientis est: ordinatio enim aliquorum fieri non potest nisi per cognitionem habitudinis et proportionis ordinatorum ad invicem et ad aliquid altius eius, quod est *finis* eorum; ordo enim aliquorum ad invicem est propter ordinem eorum ad *finem." Cont. Gent.,* II, 24.

[72]Cf. chapter two, note 58.

[73]". . . toute la théologie (et la révélation et la foi) se réfèrent à ce double objet: Dieu béatifiant, l'économie divine des moyens de la béatitude, c'est-à-dire, encore au double mystère de Dieu: le mystère nécessaire de sa vie trinitaire et le mystère libre de notre salut par l'incarnation rédemptrice." Congar, "Théologie," cols. 457-58.

[74]Cf. *Summa* I, q. 1, a. 1, c.

[75]"Si la science sacrée se développait dans une autre direction, elle ne serait bientôt plus la science du salut et de la sanctification." J. Vacant, *Etudes théologiques sur les Constitutions du Concile du Vatican* (Paris: Delhomme et Briguet, 1895), p. 224.

[76]Cf. Congar, "Théologie," col. 454.

Theology, like metaphysics, is linked with happiness, for it is a "habit of acquired wisdom whose act is contemplative happiness."[77] Here again, the very object of happiness is possessed, but now as better known in the intimacy of revealed truth. The theologian confronts an object of knowledge, it is true, but God is more than an object of knowledge. He is the theologian's final *raison d'être,* and attaining him in contemplation as he reveals himself is a far different experience from that of the metaphysician. In a much more profound sense theological wisdom and its contemplation give to man a "certain beginning or participation of future happiness."[78] The hierarchical view realized in theological contemplation presents God and reality in their supernatural affinity. Creation is for grace, nature is for supernature, and the contact with God as ultimate supernatural end brings with it a sense of arrival and an experience of the happiness found in possessing God.

For man, who has not yet arrived finally, who in the dynamism of passing time knows the profound insecurity of his position, the contemplation of God as end does two things. In a certain sense it places the theologian, however temporarily and imperfectly, in possession of his ultimate end, but at the same time it suggests the problem of the means necessary to make that

---

[77]". . . habitum sapientiae acquisitae cujus actus est felicitas contemplativa." *In II Sent.,* D. 41, q. 1, a. 1, sol.

[78]". . . quaedam inchoatio seu participatio futurae felicitatis." *Summa* I-II, q. 66, a. 5, ad 2. Cf. the following remarks of a contemporary writer: "La théologie émane de la foi; elle naît en elle et par elle. Elle naît de sa débilité, de la débilité radicale qu'est pour un esprit l'assentiment à des propositions qu'il ne voit ni mesure. Mais elle naît aussi de sa puissance, de cette puissance qu'emmagasine dans une âme en quête de possession la perception réaliste de la réalité divine mystérieuse, *substantia rerum sperandarum.* L'acte du croyant ne se termine pas en effet à la proposition dogmatique, mais à la réalité divine même qu'elle exprime humainement. Non pas donc un concept, des formules, un système de pensée; mais Celui en qui je reconnais le tout de ma vie, l'objet délectable de mon bonheur. La foi certes est assentiment à des propositions, véhicules authentiques de sa perception religieuse; mais c'est sa misère cela, ou plutôt la misère provisoire de mon esprit, qui ne connaît la vérité, même divine, que dans des propositions. Elle est à travers cela, et grâce à cela, adhésion à ce qui accomplit tous les désirs, l'unique désir de mon âme: la béatitude dans le don de Dieu même." Chenu, *Une école,* pp. 58-59.

possession permanent. As the reflection of God's own knowledge, theology is not only speculative, but also practical; it views not only God in his Trinitarian life and the entire created order proceeding from him, but also the return, the movement of man back to his Creator. What this implies shall be discussed later. For the moment, our concern is an analysis of the affective dimension in theological contemplation.

3. *Theological Contemplation and Affectivity*

Any serious mention of the affective order in theology recalls immediately the tradition of controversy, seen in the opposition of what is called Augustinianism and Thomism. The opposition seems based in misunderstanding, for the mutual criticism, of anti-intellectualism on the one hand, and of rationalism on the other, fails to recognize the ultimate ordination of speculative study to what St. Albert the Great called *veritas affectiva beatificans*.[79] We have already seen this realized in metaphysics, where the recognition of final cause should engage the personality beyond the mere attraction to a perfecting act. God, as the object of wisdom's contemplation, unlike lesser objects of knowledge, commits the wise man to the affective order. In theology, however, this commitment is immeasurably more profound than its counterpart in metaphysics.

Theology receives its principles from faith, whose roots are nourished by an essential affectivity. The assent made by the intellect to revealed truth depends upon a movement of the will.[80] Here, in its very inception, because of its subordination to faith, theology is colored with affective tones. And since faith is everywhere operative throughout the rational construction of revelation, there must be an affective note running through the entire structure. This supernatural affectivity in

[79]*In I Sent.*, D. 1, a. 4, 3m (cited by Chenu, *Théologie comme science*, p. 99.).
[80]Cf. above, section I A, on the assent to revelation. Besides the texts cited there, see also: *In III Sent.*, D. 23, q. 2, a. 3, q1a. 1, 2m; *In Boet. De Trin.*, q. 3, a. 1, 4m; *De Ver.*, q. 14, a. 2, 10m and 13m; a. 4, c; *Cont. Gent.*, III, 40; *Summa* II-II, q. 2, a. 1, c.

theology reaches its fullness in the act of contemplation, where God is attained by the mind and loved and enjoyed by the will. Faith itself, therefore, introduces the affective order in theology.[81]

The initial and terminal affectivity, distinguished in the discussion of metaphysical contemplation, qualified now by the supernatural, adds even greater force to theology's link with the affective. The love of the contemplative act and of its object, now known more intimately, gives birth to a two-fold delight. But as before, to be fully meaningful, the love of the object must be primary, without which the affective dimension in contemplation loses its significance. It is a question of engaging the entire personality, and this is possible only in the attachment to the object itself as ultimate final cause. God must be loved, not only the act of contemplating him. He must ultimately be loved supernaturally, and this demands charity, without which theological contemplation is incomplete.[82] If the whole man is involved in wisdom, here in the supernatural order the essential commitment of man's will is required and can only be realized in charity. Wisdom's primary act—*to contemplate divine things loved*[83]—is meaningless without charity. All this is not meant to make charity essential to theology. While it is a truism to say that faith is essential to theology— without certain principles there can be no theology, unless it be a mere formal dialectic—it would be false to suggest that

[81]Although faith begins in the will, the affectivity involved is not necessarily charity: "Inchoatio etiam fidei est in affectione, inquantum voluntas determinat intellectum ad assentiendum his quae sunt fidei. Sed illa voluntas nec est actus caritatis nec spei sed quidam appetitus boni repromissi." *De Ver.*, q. 14, a. 2, 10m. Cf. also *Summa* II-II, q. 4, a. 7, ad 5.

[82]". . . la réflexion spéculative . . . tend à comprendre ce qui sont en elles-mêmes les réalités révélées (par l'analogie et dans le mystère); elle aboutira, normalement, si elle naît de la charité et s'y achève, à ce fruit terminal de l'activité théologique: la contemplation." Labourdette, "La théologie," p. 24.

[83]*In III Sent.*, D. 35, q. 2, a. 1, sol. 3. As remarked above, this text treats *ex professo* the gift of the Holy Spirit, but in the light of what has been said regarding metaphysical and theological contemplation, it hardly seems an invalid citation.

theology, as a perfection of the intellect, requires charity. It can be said, however, that charity is necessary for theology's integral perfection, and that theological contemplation, above all, remains seriously incomplete without charity.

The very first movement of affectivity in faith finds its perfection in charity, as the theologian surrenders himself to his ultimate final cause.[84] If the metaphysician can be involved, engaged, committed to wisdom's highest object, how much more so can the theologian. He confronts man's ultimate end in the depths, or rather, on the heights of the supernatural, where God's infinite goodness is seen in the unique substance and distinct personalities of Father, Son, and Holy Spirit. The gift of self in charity crowns the contemplation of theology with affectivity.[85] In theology, too, the "ultimate perfection of the contemplative life is realized: that divine truth not only be known, but that it also be loved."[86]

4. Theological Contemplation and Realism

The affective overtones of theological contemplation are not those of infused contemplation, but they represent, nevertheless, a real involvement of the whole personality. As in true metaphysical contemplation, all dualistic prejudices in the relationship of intellect and will lose their meaning. The realist, existential character of the affective order becomes more profoundly so, because of theology's supernatural implications. The appetitive roots of faith in the desire for happiness and the deeper affective

[84]Regarding faith as the ever-necessary basis for supernatural growth, affective as well as intellectual, the following passage is of interest: "Si, par l'adhésion à la vérité révélée, la foi se trouve au principe de tout ce qui sera progrès de notre connaissance surnaturelle de Dieu avant la vision béatifique, par ce premier engagement, de la liberté personnelle, elle est aussi principe de cette profonde et intime vie d'affections surnaturelles que d'autres vertus viendront constituer et développer, mais dont elle inclue en elle-même le premier mouvement." Labourdette, "La théologie," p. 14.

[85]"Vita contemplativa (in caritate) habet principium et finem." *Summa* II-II, q. 180, a. 8, ad 1. If this seems to refer only to mystical contemplation, it is not the case; the entire question discusses the contemplative life as involving acquired intellectual habits.

[86]". . . ultima perfectio contemplativae vitae: ut scilicet non solum divina veritas videatur sed etiam ut ametur." *Summa* II-II, q. 180, a. 7, ad 1.

tones of charity's love of friendship add warmth to the light of theological intelligence. But they do more in engaging the individual theologian existentially. The end of human life and the end of theology are really identified in the contemplative vision of God, and the imperfect participation of that vision realized in theological wisdom could hardly be more realistically important. The personal confrontation of all contemplation now means embracing the personified life and light and love of Father, Son, and Holy Spirit. Person confronts Persons, as the identification of the true and the good in wisdom's highest cause is now deepened and made rich in being realized in distinct personalities. As the theologian surrenders himself in the profound realism of supernatural friendship, the union of speculative and affective in the wisdom of theology is perfected in existential *engagement*.[87]

C. THE WISDOM OF THEOLOGY AS BOTH SPECULATIVE AND PRACTICAL

1. The Basis for Theology's Speculative-Practical Character
In treating the relation of end to theological contemplation, we saw that God is viewed not only in the necessary mystery of his Trinitarian Life, but also in the free mystery of his plan for human salvation. This dual object makes possible, even necessary, the transition of theological consideration from God as man's end and happiness to the means of attaining him. While such a transition follows the natural order of the mind,

---

[87]The glory of theology and its most profound justification are found side by side in a text filled with overtones of realism: "Inter omnia vero hominum studia sapientiae studium est perfectius, sublimius, utilius, et iucundius. Perfectius quidem, quia inquantum homo sapientiae studio dat se, intantum verae beatitudinis iam aliquam partem habet; unde Sapiens dicit, *Beatus vir qui in sapientia morabitur* (Eccli. 14:22). Sublimius autem est quia per ipsum homo praecipue ad divinam similitudinem accedit, quae *omnia in sapientia fecit* (Ps. 103: 24); unde, quia similitudo causa est dilectionis, sapientiae studium praecipue Deo per amicitiam coniungit; propter quod dicitur quod sapientia *infinitus thesaurum est hominibus, quo qui usi sunt, facti sunt participes amicitiae Dei* (Sap. 7:14). Utilius autem est quia per ipsam sapientiam ad immortalitatis regnum pervenitur: *concupiscentia enim sapientiae deducit ad regnum perpetuum* (Sap. 6:21). Iucundius autem est quia *non habet amaritudinem conversatio illius, sed laetitiam et gaudium* (Sap. 8:16)." *Cont. Gent.*, I, 2.

its basis in theology is not limited there. As an *impressio divinae scientiae,* enjoying the unique power of a higher light, theology unites the speculative and the practical, much as a superior habit contains lesser ones. St. Thomas writes:

> Sacred doctrine, existing as one, extends itself to those things which pertain to the various philosophical sciences because of the formal *ratio* under which it views diverse things, namely, insofar as they are intelligible in the divine light. For this reason, although among the philosophical sciences one may be speculative and another practical, sacred doctrine embraces both dimensions within itself, just as God in the same knowledge knows both himself and the things he has made.[88]

God, as highest truth and supreme good, becomes at the same time an object of contemplation and a rule for human acts, which take their direction from their end.[89]

While theology's higher light allows it to transcend the distinction between speculative and practical, and yet contain both eminently, it is true that it is principally speculative; "for it treats principally of divine things rather than of human acts. The latter come under its consideration to the extent that by them man is ordered to the perfect knowledge of God in which eternal happiness consists."[90] This primacy of the speculative in theology is in direct relation to the subject of faith. As St. Thomas comments, "Faith is in the speculative intellect as in a subject, as is evident from the object of faith. But because Truth itself which is the object of faith is the end of all our

[88]"Sacra doctrina, una existens, se extendit ad ea quae pertinent ad diversas scientias philosophicas propter rationem formalem quam in diversis attendit: scilicet prout sunt divino lumine cognoscibilia. Unde licet in scientiis philosophicis alia sit speculativa et alia practica, sacra autem doctrina comprehendit sub se utramque; sicut et Deus eadem scientia se cognoscit et ea quae facit." *Summa* I, q. 1, a. 4, c. Cf. also *In I Sent.,* Prol., q. 1, a. 3, sol. 1.

[89]Cf. V. Contenson, O.P., *Theologia mentis et cordis* (Coloniae Agrippinae: Metternich, 1687), I, 6a.

[90]"Magis tamen est speculativa quam practica: quia principalius agit de rebus divinis quam de actibus humanis; de quibus agit secundum quod per eos ordinatur homo ad perfectam Dei cognitionem, in qua aeterna beatitudo consistit." *Summa* I, q. 1, a. 4, c. Cf. also I, q. 1, a. 3, ad 2; *In I Sent.,* Prol., q. 1, a. 3, q1a. 1, sol. and 1m; *In Boet. De Trin.,* q. 5, a. 4, 8m.

desires and all our actions . . . hence it is that faith works through love, just as also the speculative intellect by extension becomes practical."[91]

The fact that theology, while remaining primarily speculative, is truly practical, intensifies the note of realism already discussed in relation to contemplation. If the transcendence of time in the act of theological contemplation permits the theologian to somehow attain his ultimate end, however momentarily—and nothing could be of greater importance—then the interest of theology in the means to make that attainment permanent must add to its realism.

2. *Theology and Sanctity*

To understand more clearly the implications of theological wisdom as practical, we shall examine the relationship between theology and sanctity. In what sense can it be said that sanctity and theology mutually influence one another?

First of all, in commenting upon the *Epistle to the Hebrews,* St. Thomas writes:

> The doctrine of sacred scripture contains not only truths to be considered speculatively, as in geometry, but also truths to be approved in the affective order; thus we read in Mt. 5:19: "He who observes them and teaches others to do so . . ." In other sciences, therefore, it suffices that a man be perfect according to his intellect; in this one, however, he is required to be perfect intellectually and affectively. . . . Because the truths presented in sacred scripture pertain also to the will and not only to the intellect, it is therefore necessary that the individual be perfect in both.[92]

---

[91]"Fides est in intellectu speculativo ut in subiecto: ut manifeste patet ex fidei obiecto. Sed quia veritas prima, quae est fidei obiectum, est finis omnium desideriorum et actionum nostrarum . . . inde est quod per dilectionem operatur. Sicut etiam intellectus speculativus extensione fit practicus." *Summa* II-II, q. 4, a. 2, ad 3.

[92]"Hoc enim habet sacrae scripturae doctrina, quod in ipsa non tantum traduntur speculanda, sicut in geometria, sed etiam approbanda per affectum. Unde Matt. V, 19: *Qui autem fecerit et docuerit,* etc. In aliis ergo scientiis sufficit quod homo sit perfectus secundum intellectum, in ista vero requiritur quod sit perfectus secundum intellectum et affectum . . . Et quia quae in sacra scriptura traduntur, pertinent ad affectum, et non tantum ad intellectum, ideo oportet esse perfectum in utroque." *In V Heb.,* lect. 2, no. 273.

"The doctrine of sacred scripture" is evidently theology or sacred science, for the phrase, "in other sciences," suggests the scientific character of the knowledge in question. Can this mean that sanctity is essential to theology?

To begin with, there is certainly no theology without faith. We have seen before that, deprived of certain principles, theology would degenerate into merely an elaborate dialectic, devoid of any scientific perfection. But must the faith which provides theology with its principles be living, must it be informed by charity? If what was said earlier regarding the necessity of charity in theological contemplation has any meaning, then unquestionably theology, for its perfection, requires a living faith. Otherwise, its primary act, the contemplation of God as ultimate supernatural final cause, involving a personal surrender to the object contemplated, cannot be perfectly realized. However, as already suggested, it is more accurate to speak only of theology's integral, not its essential, perfection as requiring charity. A practical science is only fully practical, integrally practical, in the actual "application of the knowledge."[93] But theology is practical, and to realize ultimately what this means demands a transition from the knowledge of virtue to the practice of virtue. The only perfect theologian would then be he who enjoys the contemplative possession of the rational structure of revelation, colored by grace and charity with dimensions of finality, affectivity, and realism, and whose life images the perfection of his vision.

All this does not mean that theology is formally charity, any more than it is formally faith; nor is it formally prudence,[94] although all these seem required to give theology its fullest essential perfection. In the words of a sixteenth-century theologian:

[93]"Sola extensio ad opus facit aliquem intellectum esse practicum." *De Ver.*, q. 14, a. 4, c.
[94]"Respondetur theologiam non esse prudentiam proxime et formaliter sed directive et architectonice . . ." John of St. Thomas, *Curs. Theol.*, In I, q. 1, Disp. 2, a. 10, no. 17 (Solesmes, I, 400).

If theology is at once speculative and practical, certainly you know that you will never have completed theology as long as you do not apply the theory to reality. Theology is the daughter of faith, which without works is dead, as well as the doctrine of that master "who began to do and to teach."[95]

If sanctity is so necessary to the full perfection of theology, it is also true that theology is, or should be, helpful to sanctity. A reciprocal causality is evident, as theology, the exemplar, paradoxically perfects its own integral formal cause.[96] This causal link between theology and human perfection is suggested by St. Thomas in these words: "This science, although it is one, is nevertheless perfect and sufficient for all human perfection because of the efficacy of the divine light. Thus it perfects man both for right action and for the contemplation of truth."[97] The science itself is perfecting, certainly not in a Socratic sense of knowledge being virtue, but rather as ordering human acts to their proper end. Theology can in no sense be isolated from the spiritual life of the individual theologian.[98] It forms a solid dogmatic and moral foundation for that life and realizes its full stature here below only in translating the affective love of its contemplation into the effective love of a virtuous life. This is not to subordinate the speculative and its corresponding affective dimension to the practical, any

[95]"Si theologia speculativa simul et practica sit, certo scias te nunquam absolutum theologiam evasurum, quandiu theoriam non reduces ad opus. Theologia est filia fidei quae sine operibus mortua est; et ejus disciplina praeceptoris qui *coepit facere et docere.*" Contenson, *Theologia mentis,* I, 6a.

[96]Although St. Thomas refers to the moral virtues as disposing causes of contemplation (*Summa* II-II, q. 180, a. 2, c.), charity, the ultimate touchstone of sanctity, is more immediately involved in contemplative perfection. Theology, however, as an exemplary cause of sanctity, does not *immediately* stimulate religious feeling, any more than the equations of thermodynamics make one feel hot or cold (Cf. Lonergan, "Theology and Understanding," p. 643).

[97]"Ista scientia, quamvis sit una, tamen perfecta est et sufficiens ad omnem humanam perfectionem propter efficacitatem divini luminis. Unde *perficit* hominem et in operatione recta et quantum ad contemplationem veritatis." *In I Sent.,* Prol., q. 1, a. 3, sol. 1.

[98]"Il n'y a aucune raison de tenir la théologie isolée chez le théologien du mouvement essentiel de sa vie chrétienne, tournée vers la possession de Dieu." Deman, "Composantes," p. 432.

more than saying that the love of God must be translated into a love of neighbor indicates a subordination of the love of God to the love of man.

What has been said above stands in direct contrast to the thought behind the modern manual practice of adding a *corollarium pietatis* at the end of each theological tract. Theology is not extrinsic to spirituality—this is the ultimate significance of its nature as eminently practical. The contemplative ordering of theological wisdom is joined here by a second realization of the maxim, *sapientis est ordinare,* as theology directs and orders human acts to their proper end.[99]

III. The Functions of Theological Wisdom

When treating the sapiential functions of metaphysics, it was pointed out that the act of contemplation is related to the other metaphysical acts either as prior or posterior to them; posterior to the demonstration of God's existence, prior to the complete judgment and defense of principles and the ordering of the lesser sciences. In theology, whose subject is God, wisdom's highest cause is already attained in the principles and, for this reason, the functions of theology regarding its principles will be discussed first. In a second section the purely demonstrative or scientific function shall be examined, followed by theology's relation to other sciences. The final paragraphs will seek to express the mystery still inherent in theological wisdom and the desire for a more immediate knowledge of God.

A. THEOLOGICAL WISDOM AND ITS PRINCIPLES

For St. Thomas, acquired wisdom is a potential whole, containing eminently the lesser intellectual perfections of understanding and science.[100] Including within itself the habit of principles

---

[99]As remarked above, prudence will be required to complete theology's remote ordination of human acts, for theology does not touch immediately the singularity of individual circumstances, which form the setting of every human act.

[100]Cf. *Summa* I-II, q. 57, a. 2, ad 2.

as a superior includes an inferior, wisdom enjoys a privileged judgment, ordering and defense of principles. But while metaphysical wisdom exercises this privilege regarding the first principles of being and knowledge, theology, presupposing a secure natural epistemology, judges, orders, and defends the supernatural first principles revealed in faith. The qualifications of both wisdoms are similar. The natural wise man is qualified in his judgment by virtue of his profound grasp of metaphysics' subject, *being*, in which all the first principles find their ultimate meaning.[101] The theologian realizes the same qualification with regard to revealed principles, because these principles are significant only in relation to *God*, the subject of theology.

When the principles of theology are identified by St. Thomas as the articles of faith, what is meant is revealed truths as distinct from rational principles, not necessarily, or exclusively, the fourteen articles of the Creed. And if the word, article, is given a special significance, it is to designate among the revealed truths those principally intended in revelation. This is not to exclude, however, the so-called *praeambula fidei* from being included among theology's principles as articles of faith.[102]

1. Unfortunately, theology's immediate consideration of principles has too often been characterized as exclusively defensive. Although the defensive function of theology, what is called today apologetics, represents a valid concern for principles, it is essentially a negative one. What is far more important is the positive concern for penetrating the sense of the mysteries involved. The analysis of terms, recourse to analogy in the proportional unity of the natural and supernatural worlds, the comparison in confrontation of the various mysteries among themselves—these are among the primary operations of theological wisdom regarding principles. These avenues of penetration lead to the further judgment of order among the principles in hierarchical interdependence and serve the contemplative

---

[101]Cf. *Summa* I-II, q. 66, a. 5, ad 4. See also chapter two, note 82.
[102]Cf. Deman, "Composantes," p. 419, note 1.

vision spoken of earlier.[103] *Sapientis est ordinare* finds here a third realization, as the theologian orders the revealed principles of his wisdom.

In ranging the articles of faith hierarchically, the highest rank is given to the two-fold mystery of God, in himself and as our happiness, suggested in the text of *Hebrews*: "Without faith it is impossible to please God. For he who comes to God must believe that God exists and is a rewarder to those that seek him."[104] Within this dual mystery in a relationship of necessary to free, as we have already seen, are found the mysteries of the Trinity and the redemptive Incarnation. Whether or not the whole of theology or in this context all its principles can be reduced to a single principle is a problem beyond the modest scope of this section on principles.[105]

2. While theology's concern for principles is primarily one of analysis and explication, of judgment and comparative evaluation, it does involve also the function of defense. As wisdom, theology is supreme in its order, which gives to it both the prerogative and the obligation to defend its own principles. According to St. Thomas:

> Since theology has no superior, it must dispute with anyone who denies its principles. The basis for argument is divine revelation, i.e., if the opponent accepts that revelation—as in disputing with heretics we employ the authoritative texts of sacred doctrine and with those who deny one article of faith

[103]"L'essentiel est, pour la théologie, d'analyser, déduire, pour mieux pénétrer le sens et la portée des vérités premières de la religion renfermées dans le *Credo*, et parvenir aussi au simple regard, à la vue très simple de ces vérités, prégnantes de toutes les autres vérités." J. Bonnefoy, O.F.M., "La théologie comme science et l'explication de la foi selon Saint Thomas d'Aquin," *Ephemerides theologicae lovaniensis*, 15 (1938), p. 494 (cited by Congar, *Bulletin thomiste*, 5 (1937-39), p. 492.).

[104]*Hebrews* 11:6. Cf. *Summa* II-II, q. 1, a. 7, c.

[105]". . . dans toute la théologie de St. Thomas l'*ipsum esse subsistens* sert de principe premier explicatif utilisé tant pour manifester les mystères que pour résoudre les difficultés qu'on leur oppose." Gagnebet, "Le problème actuel de la théologie et la science aristotélicienne," *Divus Thomas Piacenza*, 20 (1943), p. 248. Cf. the study of this problem written by N. Del Prado, O.P., *De veritate fundamentali philosophiae christianae* (Fribourg: St. Paul, 1911).

we use another article to refute them. If, however, the opponent does not accept what has been divinely revealed, there remains no way of establishing the articles of faith rationally—one can only solve whatever arguments are brought against the faith.[106]

The objective of this theological epistemology looks first to the credibility of revelation, the rational basis for accepting faith. As a prudential act, the act of faith must be reasonable and therefore requires some conviction of the fact of revelation. This is extended to the proof that some particular truth actually has been revealed. Finally, the theologian must demonstrate negatively that the mysteries of faith involve no intrinsic contradiction.

In the light of what has been said the criticism of Fr. Beumer, regarding theology's disinterest in principles, is hardly tenable. Theological wisdom is above all a study and penetration of principles, the truths revealed by God. The theologian has no other goal than the greatest possible understanding of these principles, realized in the ordered simplicity of contemplation.

B. THEOLOGY'S SCIENTIFIC OR DEMONSTRATIVE FUNCTION

When referring to theology's scientific function, even authors intent upon defending theology as a wisdom, speak of that function as though it were not sapiential.[107] It may be true that not every one of wisdom's functions is scientific; it is not true that one of them is not sapiential. While science may not be wisdom, wisdom is science. Everything in theology is

---

[106]"Sacra scriptura, cum non habeat superiorem, disputat cum negante sua principia: argumentando quidem, si adversarius aliquid concedet eorum quae per divinam revelationem habentur: sicut per auctoritates sacrae doctrinae disputamus contra hereticos, et per unum articulum contra negantes alium. Si vero adversarius nihil credat eorum quae divinitus revelantur, non remanet amplius via ad probandum articulos fidei per rationes, sed ad solvendum rationes si quas inducit, contra fidem." *Summa* I, q. 1, a. 8, c. Cf. also *In Boet. De Trin.*, q. 2, a. 3, c.; *In I Sent.*, Prol., q. 1, a. 3, sol. 2; a. 5, sol. and 4m; *Cont. Gent.*, I, 1 and 9; IV, 1; *Quodl.* IV, q. 9, a. 3; *Summa* II-II, q. 1, a. 5, ad 2.

[107]Cf. the impression given by Muniz, "De diversis muneribus," pp. 115-17.

part of the *wisdom* of theology and is, therefore, properly sapiential. To deny this, to speak of theology as though it were wisdom only in some of its functions is misleading. The properly scientific function of theology is exercised as a potential part of the one whole, the wisdom of theology. And it should be remembered that where there is question of a potential whole that whole is predicated *essentially* of each of its parts. Obviously, one must distinguish here between theology as scientific in the sense of being rational, intellectual, organized, structural, etc.—the whole of theology is scientific in this sense— and that potential part of theology which involves uniquely the function of demonstration.

The attempt to determine precisely the nature of this demonstrative function is not an easy task. In dividing any potential whole whose inferior parts are continually called into the service of their superiors a suggestion of overlapping is invariably apparent. For example, the hierarchical structuring of theology's principles referred to in the preceding section depends heavily upon judgments reached discursively. And while the truth attained in the process may be only a relation of order among the revealed truths themselves, if the reasoning has not been merely explicative it does imply a movement of science.[108] In such cases the newly gained understanding of the revealed mysteries in their relations and interrelations of order and analogy, of efficiency, exemplarity, and finality would be the

[108]Apparently Father Congar hesitates to call these insights *new* truths, for he writes: "La qualité scientifique de la théologie ne se prend pas de la déduction de vérités nouvelles, mais de la construction rationelle de l'enseignement chrétien par un rattachement de vérités-conclusions à des vérités-principes." (*Bulletin,* p. 500). It may be true that merely explicative reasoning does not, strictly speaking, attain new truth. However, when the understanding of the revealed principles in their own order is reached through properly discursive movements of the mind, how else can this be interpreted except as a discovery of new truth? On the whole question of theological demonstration see the thorough treatment given this problem by Fr. Wallace in a chapter entitled, "Prolegomena on Demonstration in Sacred Theology," in his *The Role of Demonstration in Moral Theology,* pp. 15-70.

result of theology's scientific function exercised in the area of principles.

The interest in principles is of course of the utmost importance to the theologian. The nature of his knowledge, totally dependent upon the reception of its principles in subalternation to the science of God and the blessed, demands a special concern for principles. Even more so than in metaphysics, where the self-evident principles can more or less be taken for granted. And because in all science the knowledge of conclusions depends upon seeing their foundation in the principles, the circular movement of science can never be over-emphasized. Science begins from principles only to return to them with a greater realization of their virtuality.[109] Any attempt, therefore, to limit theology's concern here to new truths completely independent of revealed principles is based upon a serious misconception. Such a mistake is evident among the critics of so-called conclusion-theology, a victim of attack which seems to have all the characteristics of a "straw man."[110] To think of the word of God only as a point of departure for theological deduction and not as the ultimate objective of theology's scientific function

---

[109]The texts of two contemporary authors are worth citing here: "La ciencia puede ser tal si sólo es de las conclusiones? Es que un saber puede abandonar sus fundamentos? . . . Luego el 'scientia est conclusionum' no querra décir un abandono de los principios, una consideración absoluta de ellos, ya que esto es imposible, si es verdad que en ellos encuentran su razón de ser las conclusiones. Su sentido exacto será que el concepto de 'scientia,' en cuanto contrapuesto al de 'intellectus,' queda determinado por las conclusiones y no por los principios que definen únicamente al 'intellectus.'" J. M. Alonzo, C.M.F., "La teologia como ciencia," *Revista española de teologia,* 5 (1945), p. 628. (Cf. the bibliography on the problem of theology as science, pp. 3-6); and "Come è possibile, infatti, dedurre conclusioni vere e proprie, che spieghino il reale ricco contenuto dei principi rivelati, se non approfondendo la conoscenza dei principi stessi, con lo studiarne seriamente le fonti, cioè la S. Scrittura e la Tradizione che nei Padri ha il suo canale sacro?" Daffara, "La teologia," p. 18.

[110]"Fausse conception de la finalité du labeur théologique qui serait déduire des conclusions des propositions de la foi. Non, la théologie en tant que science spéculative a pour fin la connaissance de son sujet qui est Dieu, et en tant que science pratique l'obtention de Dieu, notre fin surnaturelle." Gagnebet, "Dieu sujet de la théologie," p. 54.

99

betrays a false set of values and a mistaken notion of the meaning of science.[111]

We have said that theology's demonstrative function may be realized as it serves immediately the function regarding principles. If, however, the deductive processes of theological wisdom include premisses taken from natural reason conjoined to others held by faith, the demonstrative function would seem then to occupy a position more proper to itself. Yet, even here it is served by its own inferior, wisdom's function of using the lower sciences, all of which simply emphasizes the interdependence so vital among theology's various sapiential functions.

To add a note of comparative value, an important difference between philosophical and theological argumentation is pointed out by St. Thomas, which broadens the scope of the discursive process in theology: "The philosopher constructs his arguments from the proper causes of things; the theologian, however, from the first cause, as, for example, because something was divinely revealed, or because this is conducive to God's glory, or because the power of God is infinite."[112] Apparently, judging from this text, as well as from his own theological arguments in general, theology as science, for St. Thomas, must embrace the entire sweep of arguments of convenience, which induce not necessity but varying degrees of probability. Certainly the vast richness of theology, its rational construction of Christian revelation, does not depend upon demonstrative deduction in the strictest sense. "The proper and principal task of the theologian," states a modern writer, "is not limited to the fabrication of so-called virtual revelation and the work of deduction: his

[111]"La Parole de Dieu n'est pas là pour prouver des considérations théologiques, mais bien les réflexions théologiques pour pénétrer et exprimer intelligiblement la Parole de Dieu, reçue préalablement et pour elle-même dans la foi." P. Hitz, "Théologie et catéchèse," *Nouvelle revue théologique*, 87 (1955), pp. 908-09 (cited by Chenu, *Théologie comme science*, p. 84, note 2.).

[112]"Nam philosophus argumentum assumit ex propriis rerum causis: fidelis autem ex causa prima; ut puta, quia sic divinitus est traditum; vel quia hoc in gloriam Dei cedit; vel quia Dei potestas est infinita." *Cont. Gent.*, II, 4.

scientific discursus, from the argument of convenience to deduction, is developed in the contemplation of revealed truth, where he knows and elaborates in a complex manner that which God knows in the absolute simplicity of an intuition."[113]

C. THEOLOGICAL WISDOM AND THE OTHER SCIENCES

If metaphysics receives certain prerogatives of authority over the lesser sciences because of its contact with ultimate final cause, theology must enjoy the same privileges with even greater reason. "Since the end of all philosophy is inferior to the end of theology and ordered to the latter, theology ought to control all the other sciences and make use of the truths presented in them."[114] The more perfect contact with ultimate final cause— God known supernaturally as he is in himself—grants to the theologian rights of judgment and order beyond those of the natural wise man.

1. As in every case of an effective superior-inferior relationship, the basis lies in the subordination of ends. A text, cited earlier in the corresponding section of metaphysical wisdom, is so important here, it deserves a second introduction. St. Thomas writes: "The ultimate perfection of the human intellect is divine truth; other truths perfect the intellect as ordered toward divine truth."[115] All human knowledge is meant to lead man to knowledge of God. Such a statement, of course, should not be interpreted in too Platonic a sense, seeing lesser realities

---

[113]". . . la tâche propre et principale du théologien, qui n'est pas bloquée sur la fabrication du 'révélé virtuel,' comme on dit, et sur le travail de déduction: son discursus scientifique, depuis l'argument de convenance jusqu'à la déduction, se construit dans la contemplation même du donné révélé, où il connaît et élabore à sa manière complexe ce que Dieu connaît dans la simplicité absolue d'une intuition." Chenu, *Théologie comme science,* p. 89. The sense given here to the phrase, "révélé virtuel," is obviously quite limited. As we have seen before, virtual revelation, as the formal object of theology, can and should be given a broader interpretation, beyond the restrictions of the strict demonstrative process.

[114]"Cum finis totius philosophiae sit infra finem theologiae, et ordinatus ad ipsum, theologia debet omnibus aliis scientiis imperare et uti his quae in eis traduntur." *In I Sent.,* Prol., q. 1, a. 1, sol.

[115]"Ultima perfectio humani intellectus est veritas divina: aliae autem veritates perficiunt intellectum in ordine ad veritatem divinam." *Summa* II-II, q. 180, a. 4, ad 4.

A *theology of wisdom*

as mere reflections of the divine and not as having real, existential value in themselves. There is essential terminal value in lesser beings, as well as in the knowledge of them. But everything is ultimately ordered to God, and in this sense all knowledge, too, shares the same ordination. This is why the integration of academic curricula is a function of wisdom, as mentioned earlier in the section on metaphysics. Here, of course, it is seen as a task proper to the theologian.[116]

As in metaphysics theology's ordering of the lower sciences can never be valid without respect for the intrinsic autonomy of each science. If being dogmatic and doctrinaire is out of place for the theologian elsewhere, here, above all, it cannot be tolerated. Unlike metaphysics theology does not even prove the principles of the other sciences: "It does not belong to theology to prove the principles of other sciences but only to judge them: whatever is found in other sciences to be repugnant to the truth of this science is to be wholly condemned as false."[117] The judgment exercised by theology simply approves the conformity of another science's conclusions with revealed truth. Since God is the author of all truth, there can be no possibility of something true contradicting what he has revealed. This negative watch of the theologian over the deposit of faith is at the same time a control over the lower sciences and a necessary counterpart of the defensive function regarding principles discussed earlier.

2. Perhaps more important in theology's relation to other sciences is its right to make use of their conclusions. Following the judgment of the lesser disciplines according to his higher

116The argument set forth by Cardinal Newman in the admirable early chapters of his *Idea of a University* might have been strengthened by such an allusion to theology's role in ordering educational curricula. For more on that relationship cf. T. Donlan, O.P., *Theology and Education* (Dubuque: The Priory Press, 1952); and V. E. Smith, *The School Examined —Its Aim and Content* (Milwaukee: Bruce, 1960).

117"Non pertinet ad eam probare principia aliarum scientiarum, sed solum iudicare de eis: quidquid est in aliis scientiis invenitur veritati huius scientiae repugnans, totum condemnatur ut falsum." *Summa* I, q. 1, a. 6, ad 2.

criterion of truth, the subordination of ends grants to the theologian the right to use whatever truths in those disciplines will serve his end: "Theology uses all the other sciences as handmaids in its service."[118] Theology is interested here, not by reason of necessity, but because the greater evidence of natural truths leads the mind more connaturally to understand revealed truths.[119] Throughout the appropriation of rational premises in theological wisdom, however, the absolute primacy of faith and the supernatural is never lessened. Natural truths enter as instruments of faith's principal causality and enjoy an elevated position.[120] The water is changed into wine in St. Thomas's well-known figure.[121]

In evaluating the position of theology with reference to other sciences the maxim, *sapientis est ordinare*, cannot be realized in quite the same way as it is in metaphysics. Because metaphysics justifies the principles of the lesser sciences, it orders them more immediately than does theology. The negative check of confrontation with revealed doctrine and the use of truths found in the lower sciences ultimately characterize this particular sapiential function of theological wisdom. Is there an ordering? Significantly, yes, for theology orders all lesser knowledge to its own sublime end of contemplating God.

[118]"(Theologia) utitur in obsequium sui omnibus aliis scientiis quasi vassallis . . ." *In I Sent.*, Prol., q. 1, a. 1, sol. Cf. also *In Boet. De Trin.*, q. 2, a. 3, 7m; *Cont. Gent.*, II, 4; *Summa* I, q. 1, a. 5, ad 2.

[119]"Haec scientia accipere potest aliquid a philosophicis disciplinis, non quod ex necessitate eis indigeat, sed ad maiorem manifestationem eorum quae in hac scientia traduntur. Non enim accipit sua principia ab aliis scientiis, sed immediate a Deo per revelationem. Et ideo non accipit ab aliis scientiis tanquam a superioribus, sed utitur eis tanquam inferioribus et ancillis; sicut architectonicae utuuntur subministrantibus, ut civilis militari. Et hoc ipsum quod sic utitur eis, non est propter defectum vel insufficientiam eius, sed propter defectum intellectus nostri; qui ex eis quae per naturalem rationem (ex qua procedunt aliae scientiae) cognoscuntur, facilius manuducitur in ea quae sunt supra rationem, quae in hac scientia traduntur." *Summa* I, q. 1, a. 5, ad 2.

[120]Cf. John of St. Thomas, *Curs. Theol.*, In I, q. 1, Disp. 2, a. 6, no. 8 (Solesmes, I, 370). "La prémisse naturelle n'exerce pas dans le raisonnement théologique la fonction d'une cause principale agissant par sa vertu propre. Mais elle y entre à titre d'instrument . . ." Gagnebet, "La nature," p. 32.

[121]*In Boet. De Trin.*, q. 2, a. 3, 5m.

D. THE INCOMPLETENESS OF THEOLOGICAL WISDOM

Natural human wisdom, knowing God only in his creatures, terminates in desire, as it contemplates in essential ignorance the mystery of infinite being. The object of that desire: to know from within something of the first cause. As man is introduced to the higher world of the supernatural through the gift of faith, God is known from within. But the knowledge of faith remains mysterious. Though it is true that "the act of one who believes does not terminate in the proposition but in the thing,"[122] the conceptual formula is always the indispensable medium through which faith must pass. As conceptual, faith obscures the divine reality in the limitations of finite concepts, and this obscurity is communicated to theology. The mystery of God, though revealed now from within, rests hidden, and there is realized again the truth of the statement: "At the term of our knowledge we are said to know God as one unknown."[123]

The wisdom of theology, like that of metaphysics, must also end in desire. The mediate knowledge of faith guards the mystery of ultimate cause in conceptual chains which bind the theologian. In this opaque world where vision is impossible the wise man desires to be freed from his conceptual bonds to enjoy a more immediate knowledge of God, a more perfect contemplation, a higher wisdom.[124]

[122]"Actus credentis non terminatur ad enuntiabile sed ad rem." *Summa* II-II, q. 1, a. 2, ad 2.

[123]*In Boet. De Trin.*, q. 1, a. 2, 1m. Cf. also the texts cited above in chap. 2, note 100, as well as the illuminating work of Victor White, O.P., *God the Unknown and Other Essays* (New York: Harper & Bros., 1956).

[124]"(La contemplation théologique) n'est assurément pas encore la contemplation infuse, mais cette réalisation analogique de la notion de contemplation qui se trouve au terme de toute vraie *sagesse,* dès que celle-ci s'inspire de l'amour et y conduit . . . . elle ne saurait être 'terminale' . . . elle ouvre le désir d'une connaissance supérieure, elle sent elle-même le besoin de laisser la place à la contemplation infuse, ou du moins de se couronner en elle, de se laisser diriger par elle. Et ce sera alors pour l'esprit du croyant une nouvelle 'intelligence de la foi,' mais dont le Saint-Esprit a seul en lui l'initiation." Labourdette, "La théologie," p. 44.

IV

THE WISDOM OF THE
HOLY SPIRIT

In the preceding chapters we have discussed two distinct wisdoms, two acquired contemplative habits, metaphysics and theology. In the present chapter we are no longer concerned with acquisitions of reason which attain God in the natural and supernatural orders and whose acts are controlled by the will. Here we leave the realm of the active to enter a less familiar world of passivity. Our attention moves from the acquired to the infused, from the conceptual to the supra-conceptual, from the human to the divine. Is there a wisdom higher than either metaphysics or theology which can be realized in man? If so, what is the nature of that wisdom and what are its characteristics? These are the questions to be considered in the following pages, the *an sit, quid sit,* and *qualis sit* of wisdom, gift of the Holy Spirit.

I. WISDOM, ONE OF SEVEN DISTINCT GIFTS?

As the problem of metaphysics' existence was qualified to concern the approach to the study of being, presupposed to be a valid branch of study, here, too, the *an sit* of infused wisdom will be qualified. With the preponderance of traditional Christian sources testifying unquestionably to gifts of the Holy Spirit, cognitive, as well as affective, the consideration at hand will

A theology of wisdom

investigate primarily the existence of wisdom as a distinct gift, one among precisely seven.

The traditional enumeration of seven gifts finds its Scriptural basis in the well-known text of Isaias: "And the Spirit of the Lord shall rest upon him: the spirit of *wisdom* and of *understanding*, the spirit of *counsel* and of *fortitude*, the spirit of *knowledge* and of *piety;* and he shall be filled with the spirit of the *fear of the Lord*."[1] This text, however, though apparently a basis for seven gifts, indicates only six in the Hebrew original. According to most exegetes, the number, seven, has come down to us through the Septuagint and St. Jerome.[2] Nevertheless, tradition has sanctified the number, seven, and Christian theology has continued to speculate upon and dispute the exact meaning of each gift.[3] Whether or not this number, seven, is meant to signify seven specifically distinct gifts, or simply a certain plenitude, will be studied more closely below.

From the Old Testament enumeration and the New Testament allusions to inspired Christian activity[4], through the writings of the Fathers[5] and the liturgy[6], to the doctrine of Trent[7] and Pope Leo XIII[8], the existence of certain gifts, bestowed by the

[1]*Isa.* 11:2.

[2]Cf. E. Power in *A Catholic Commentary on Holy Scripture* (London: Thos. Nelson & Sons, 1953), p. 550, no. 428m.

[3]Cf. the scriptural and historical section of the article, "Dons du Saint-Esprit," written by A. Gardeil in the *Dictionnaire de théologie catholique*, T. IV, col. 1748-79. See also F. Utz, O.P., "Kommentar über I-II, q. 68" in *Die Deutsche Thomas-Aufgabe: Summa theologica*, Bd. 11 (Salzburg: Pustet, 1940), pp. 630-51.

[4]Among New Testament texts, confer: *Mt.* 11:25-26; *Jn.* 14:21,23; 15:26, 17:26; *Rom.* 8:15, 26,27; *1 Cor.* 2:6-16; 6:19; *2 Cor.* 3:18; 6:16; *Eph.* 3:17-19; *Phil.* 1:9; *1 Jn.* 2:27. Most of these texts suggest a special, divinely inspired knowledge, a wisdom of the Spirit (Cf. Journet, *Connaissance*, pp. 119-23). For the scriptural basis of the gifts, see also John of St. Thomas, *Curs. Theol.*, In I-II, q. 68-70, Disp. 18, a. 1 (Laval, nos. 22-93).

[5]For a conspectus of doctrine on the gifts in the Fathers, cf. Gardeil, "Dons," cols. 1754-71. See also L. Roy, S.J., *Lumière et sagesse* (Montréal: L'Immaculée Conception, 1948), pp. 135-54.

[6]The important liturgical sources are the two hymns to the Holy Spirit, found in the Liturgy of Pentecost: the *Veni Sancte Spiritus* and the *Veni Creator Spiritus*.

[7]Denz. 799.

[8]*Divinum Illud* in *Acta sanctae sedis*, 29 (1896-97), pp. 644-58.

Holy Spirit upon the individual in grace, finds sufficient confirmation. The doctrine becomes more problematic, however, when theology seeks to determine the precise nature of the gifts (Are they really identified with the supernatural virtues? How necessary are they for salvation? Are they acts or habits?) and their precise number. These were the problems raised by the scholastic theologians who preceded St. Thomas.[9] In the paragraphs that follow a brief presentation of his doctrine on the gifts in general will be given, together with a discussion of the numerical problem. This should provide the necessary background for the analysis of infused wisdom's nature and properties.

A. ST. THOMAS AND THE GIFTS

Presupposing the existence of the gifts as a legacy from scripture and tradition, St. Thomas examines successively their distinction from the moral virtues, their necessity, and their nature as habits, before attempting to determine a precise function for each gift.[10] The gifts, he says, because they involve inspiration, suggest "a certain movement from without."[11] This implies a mover other than reason, the interior principle of human activity. While man is moved interiorly by reason, he is moved exteriorly by God. And as he is disposed for the movement of reason by the moral virtues, similarly, the gifts dispose him for the

[9]Cf. O. Lottin, O.S.B., *Psychologie et morale au XIIe et XIIIe siècles* (Louvain: Abbaye de Mont César, 1942-54), III, 329-411.

[10]St. Thomas presents his doctrine on the gifts in general in *In III Sent.*, D. 34, in *Summa* I-II, q. 68, and in the commentary on *Isaias*, c. 11. The summary presented here follows the order found in *Summa* I-II, q. 68. Cf. Roy, *Lumière*, pp. 155-96, for a comparative study of St. Thomas's position as reflected in these texts.

[11]". . . quandam motionem ab exteriori." *Summa* I-II, q. 68, a. 1, c. As Cajetan comments, regarding the various principles of human activity: "In homine est triplex subordinatum movens ad actus bonos: scilicet mens humana praedita lumine naturali et prudentia; mens humana praedita lumine gratiae et fidei; et mens humana pulsata instinctu Spiritus Sancti. Et ad hoc ut vires animae obediant primo motori, ponuntur virtutes morales acquisitae, tendentes ad media et fines ab ipso motore praestitutos. Ad hoc autem ut eaedem vires obediant secundo motori superiori, ponuntur virtutes morales infusae, tendentes ad media et fines ab illo motore praestitutos. Ad hoc autem quod non solum eaedem, sed omnes vires animae obediant supremo motori, ponuntur supremo dona, tendentia in fines proprios a tali motore ostendos." *Commentaria in Summam Theologiae*, I-II, 68, 1, no. 3. Cf. also Marin-Sola, *L'évolution*, I, 389.

divine motion. A duality of moving principles, consequently, is the basis for distinguishing the gifts from the moral virtues.

To demonstrate the necessity of the gifts, St. Thomas bases his argument upon the disproportion between man's supernatural end and his means of attaining that end. With only reason as a moving principle even the supernatural perfection of the theological virtues is not enough to assure success. These latter, having for their object God in his intimate nature, can be possessed by man only imperfectly and, therefore, cannot insure adequately his supernatural orientation. They require the protection and perfection of a higher mover, the divine instinct of the Holy Spirit.[12] The obscurity of faith's judgment regarding God in himself is communicated to charity, and the consequent imperfection of our knowledge and love of God creates a need for divine assistance over and above that provided by the infused virtues.

St. Thomas goes on to prove that the gifts are infused as habits, disposing man in a permanent manner for the motion of the Spirit. His reasoning here does not enjoy the demonstrative force of the preceding proof; it is, rather, an argument from convenience or fittingness, based upon the analogy between the natural and supernatural orders. If the appetitive powers are disposed by habits, the moral virtues, to receive the commands of reason, it should follow that the supernatural dispositions, which make the entire man docile to divine inspiration, have also the perfection of being habits. Otherwise, human nature would be more perfectly prepared for its natural operations than for those operations whose ultimate importance is far more vital. Natural morality would be better assured than supernatural morality. The dialectical force of such reasoning is evident, but because the divine motion, strictly speaking, could be realized without abiding dispositions in the subject, the argumentation seems probable rather than necessary.[13]

[12]Cf. *Summa* I-II, q. 68, a. 2, c.
[13]Cf. Gardeil, "Dons," col. 1737: "A la rigueur ils peuvent ne pas l'être (habitus)."

B. THE PROBLEM OF SEVEN GIFTS

Of special interest in this introductory section is the problem concerning the number of the gifts. Is the wisdom of the Holy Spirit a habit totally distinct from the gifts of understanding and science, or are these three intellectual dispositions part of a seven-fold enumeration, signifying plenitude rather than distinction? Are there precisely seven gifts of the Holy Spirit, or many more, or perhaps only two, one intellectual, the other appetitive?[14]

St. Thomas gives the impression that he considers the number seven somewhat definitive, although he is certainly aware of that number's symbolic signification.[15] But in his classification of the seven gifts he may have been simply following the scholastic practice of systematizing what had been handed down by tradition. Whether or not St. Thomas himself really thought there were exactly seven gifts, no more, no less, is extremely problematic. The surface evidence, it is true, seems to support an affirmative response, but other considerations qualify considerably the certitude of such a response.

We have seen that the scriptural basis for seven gifts is doubtful, with the original Hebrew indicating only six. St. Thomas, of course, being unaware of this, would have been inclined to accept seven less critically than would have been the case had he known the Isaias original. As a result, he was led to conjecture upon the proper acts of each of the seven gifts. In doing so, he changed his opinion three times. The organization of the gifts is presented in four different texts, and in each presentation the analysis is different.[16] Is one

---

[14]Such questions would be dismissed categorically by John of St. Thomas, for whom "non dubitari potest de numero donorum quod septem sint . . . nulla probabilitas relinqui possit in sententia opposita." *Curs. Theol.*, In I-II, q. 68-70, Disp. 18, a. 7, nos. 1 and 2 (Laval, nos. 1028 and 1032).

[15]"Septenarius universitatem significat," *Summa* I-II, q. 102, a. 5, ad 5. For other texts, cf. Roy, *Lumière*, pp. 175-77.

[16]*In III Sent.*, D. 34, q. 1, a. 2; *Summa* I-II, q. 68, a. 4; II-II, q. 8, a. 6, c.; *In Isaiam*, c. 11. On this problem, cf. Roy, *Lumière*, pp. 174-86, 295-96.

of them definitive? Depending on the chronology of St. Thomas's works, either the text in the *Secunda-Secundae* of the *Summa Theologiae* or the one in the commentary on *Isaias* represents his final opinion. Neither is particularly convincing, although the text in the *Summa* reflects greater probability.[17] The appetitive gifts, piety, fortitude, and fear, submit to rather facile categorization in the will and the irascible and concupiscible appetites. Even counsel seems secure in the practical intellect. But the problem is compounded when one attempts to distinguish the other intellectual gifts, wisdom, understanding, and science, among themselves.

It must be remembered that St. Thomas was compelled to invert the normal order in psychology, which determines the nature of a habit by studying first the object of the act. Here, St. Thomas was given the habits, for which he then had to assign proper acts and objects. Assuming that the seven gifts were seven distinct realities, he ingeniously isolated acts and objects proper to each. But was he completely successful? Without the assurance of revelation to the effect that each gift is a distinct reality, as a modern author points out, the only basis for distinguishing the gifts would be through recourse to analogy with the natural order.[18] But it is precisely here that the differentiation made among the three intellectual gifts, mentioned above, falls short. Why limit wisdom to divine things and science to created things, when natural wisdom implies a consideration of all things in view of highest causes? If the gifts bring with them divine inspiration at a supernatural level,

[17]The statement of Gardeil, regarding St. Thomas's defense of the order followed by Isaias in enumerating the gifts, seems equally applicable here. Influenced by a profound respect for antiquity, he says, St. Thomas presents reasons for that particular order, but, "ces considérations paraîtront peut-être plus ingénieuses que justifiées." in "Dons," col. 1741. The conceptual gymnastics become even more remarkable when the beatitudes and fruits of the Holy Spirit are individually linked with the various gifts. In such a context it is difficult not to conjecture in terms of this alternative: either St. Thomas was more a creature of his age than many of us are wont to admit, or else he wrote a few lines of his *Summa* with "tongue-in-cheek."

[18]Roy, *Lumière*, p. 185.

all judgments will be made in the light of the divine, and ultimately referred to God.[19] In the natural order the plurality of sciences makes meaningful the distinction between science and wisdom, but inspired knowledge, the *scientia sanctorum*, does not connote this multiplicity. As a matter of fact, since the gifts effect a higher, more divine kind of knowledge, it would seem more fitting that the intellectual gifts, as more perfect images of God's knowledge, be as few as possible.[20] Wisdom and understanding would be enough. However, if understanding in the natural order only adheres by assent to first principles, while wisdom penetrates their deeper significance, why alter this relationship in reference to the gifts?[21] Therefore, perhaps wisdom alone would suffice.[22] Further, by pointing out the extent of the practical dimension of infused wisdom it is possible that a distinct gift of counsel might be eliminated; the inspired judgment of means would already be accounted for.

The remarks above are not meant to be conclusive. In a field of study as obscure as is the theology of the gifts it is difficult, if not impossible, to surpass the limits of a more or

[19]St. Thomas himself attributes this dual judgment to the gift of wisdom, which "facit rectitudinem iudicii circa res divinas vel per regulas divinas de aliis." *Summa* II-II, q. 45, a. 4, c. Cf. also a. 3, c.

[20]From another point of view, a similar question is posed, but apparently answered satisfactorily: "Pourquoi une seule science théologique par une dialectique ascendante et descendante (non exclusivement ascendante comme le don de science ou descendante comme le don de sagesse) suffit-elle pour juger de la fin dernière et des moyens d'y parvenir, alors que la connaissance expérimentale mystique, cependant suprème, se fait sur les mêmes domaines par les dons multiples d'intelligence, de science, de sagesse et de conseil, nous ne pouvons le dire par le seul raisonnement humain. Nous devons nous en tenir à la révélation des sept dons." Philipon, "La théologie," p. 409. But the question remains, does revelation confirm the existence of seven formally distinct gifts?

[21]Cf. for example, *In III Sent.*, D. 35, q. 2, a. 1, q1a. 1, 1m: "Sicut se habet sapientia quae est virtus intellectualis ad intellectum principiorum . . . ita se habet sapientia quae est donum ad *fidem* quae est cognitio simplex articulorum."

[22]This is not to suggest merely that wisdom includes "eminentiori modo" the perfections of understanding and science. It is, rather, a conjectured denial of the possibility of a distinct gift of understanding, different from the simple assent made to supernatural truth by faith, and of science, which at the level of the gifts seems to be completely absorbed by the gift of wisdom. Do the latter two really have a necessary *raison d'être?*

less well-founded dialectic.[23] The question, whether or not St. Thomas really believed that the gifts were seven distinct realities, will not be answered categorically.[24] The discussion above was included simply to prepare the way for an examination of infused wisdom's nature and properties. It was meant to make possible later statements, which may seem to attribute to the wisdom of the Spirit characteristics apparently proper to understanding and science in the mind of St. Thomas. If the word, *wisdom*, as signifying a gift, however, is not to be lost in complete equivocation, traits considered belonging to it in its acquired analogates will be considered also proper to it here.[25]

II. The Nature of the Gift of Wisdom and Its Primary Act

As before, an affirmative response to the question, *an sit*, invites, even demands, the further determination of the *quid sit*. Presupposing, therefore, the existence of infused wisdom, together with the qualifications presented above, regarding the problem of a distinct intellectual gift among others, the present section

---

[23]"In der Bestimmung und Zuteilung der Gaben lässt sich überall eine gewisse Unsicherheit feststellen." Utz, "Kommentar," p. 646. But another contemporary writer holds for "la plus haute probabilité" in the sevenfold enumeration of the gifts. Cf. M.-M. Philipon, "Les dons du Saint-Esprit," *Revue thomiste*, 61 (1961), p. 254.

[24]According to a modern commentator: "Die erwünschte Einheit und Geschlossenheit im Traktat über die Gaben des Heiligen Geistes wäre vielleicht besser geglückt, wenn Thomas die Isaiasstelle nicht mit so viel Rücksicht behandelt hätte wie seine Vorzeit, sondern die Siebenzahl mit vielen Vätern einfach als Ausdruck der Fülle genommen und entsprechend auch die Namengebung nicht als zwingend angesehen hätte." Utz, "Kommentar," p. 650.

[25]When St. Thomas says that wisdom, as referring to acquired and infused wisdom, is equivocal, the word, *equivocal*, must signify analogous. (*In III Sent.*, D. 34, q. 1, a. 1, 1m; D. 35, q. 2, a. 1, q1a. 1, 3m). He distinguishes two types of wisdom, not by denying a similarity in their common concern for ultimate cause—that is, in their formal nature—but by an appeal to diverse efficient causes: "Sapientia dicitur intellectualis virtus, secundum quod procedit ex iudicio rationis; dicitur autem donum, secundum quod operatur ex instinctu divino." *Summa* I-II, q. 68, a. 1, ad 4.

will comprise three topics: 1) infused wisdom as affective knowledge; 2) contemplation as its principal or primary act; and 3) the speculative-practical character of that wisdom.

A. WISDOM AS AFFECTIVE KNOWLEDGE

It is evident that if man is to receive the motion of a superior mover, he must be united to that mover in some way. Consequently, because the gifts dispose man to receive the moving inspiration of the Holy Spirit, their entire efficacy depends upon the individual's being united to the Holy Spirit. This union, however, while effected by all the theological virtues—their proper object is God—is made perfect only by charity. Unlike faith, which requires a conceptual medium, and hope, which looks to God not yet possessed, charity attains God immediately and is united to him as already possessed; "for the one loved is somehow in the lover and the lover is drawn by affectivity into union with the one loved."[26] Without charity there is no living, effective union with God, which forms the indispensable basis for the gifts. This means that each of the gifts, because fundamentally based in the union of charity, is radically affective. The gift of wisdom, therefore, introduces an affectivity far more intrinsic to the knowledge involved than the affectivity seen earlier in connection with acquired wisdom. As the disposition to judge ultimate causality through inspirations rooted in charity, wisdom seems to be a form of what is called affective knowledge. But this must be examined more critically.

1. The Nature of Affective Knowledge

St. Thomas apparently gives a double interpretation to the notion, affective knowledge. In some instances it signifies a

---

[26]"Est enim amatum quodammodo in amante, et etiam amans per affectum trahitur ad unionem amati." *Summa* I-II, q. 66, a. 6, c. "Qui manet in caritate, in Deo manet," adds St. Thomas, citing 1 Jn. 4:16. The question on the effects of love, *Summa* I-II, q. 28, especially articles 1 and 2, contains remarkable insights on this uniting force of love.

A *theology of wisdom*

knowledge which produces love[27]; in others, a knowledge produced by love, that is, one that is formally affective.[28] Although both these interpretations, as we shall see below, are applicable to the wisdom of the Spirit, the second is primary—infused wisdom is formally affective knowledge. Before we can understand precisely what this means, two aspects of the problem must be studied. Each concerns the relationship which obtains between the intellect and the will, between knowledge and love. The first is the connaturality associated with love; the second, the immediacy of intellect and will and the consequent influence of the will's act upon the intellect.

a. Love and Connaturality

"In the life of the mind *all that is related to love,* says St. Thomas (I, 37, 1), *is especially mysterious and often beyond verbal expression,* because the intellect knows less perfectly that which is contained in another faculty than that which is in itself, and because love goes out toward the good which is in things and not in the mind; that orientation, as all that remains still undetermined, is not fully intelligible. This is one of the most

[27]"Duplex est cognitio veritatis: una quidem quae habetur per gratiam; alia vero quae habetur per naturam. Et ista quae habetur per gratiam est duplex: una quae est speculativa tantum, sicut cum alicui aliqua secreta divinorum revelatur; alia vero quae est affectiva, producens amorem Dei; et haec proprie pertinet ad donum sapientiae." *Summa* I, q. 64, a. 1, c. Cf. also I, q. 43, a. 5, ad 2.

[28]"Duplex est cognitio divinae bonitatis vel voluntatis. Una quidem speculativa . . . . Alia autem est cognitio divinae bonitatis seu voluntatis affectiva seu experimentalis, dum quis experitur in seipso gustum divinae dulcedinis et complacentiam divinae voluntatis." *Summa* II-II, q. 97, a. 2, ad 2. For a detailed comparison of these two types of knowledge, cf. Marin-Sola, *L'évolution,* I, p. 363. Distinguishing *la voie de raisonnement* from *la voie affective,* this writer lists the various expressions used by St. Thomas to signify the two. Among the expressions referring to affective knowledge are the following: a) per connaturalitatem; b) per modum inclinationis; c) cognitio affectiva; d) notitia experimentalis; e) per affinitatem (ad divina); f) per modum naturae; g) per viam voluntatis; h) per contactum; i) per unionem (ad Deum); j) per amorem; k) ex intimo sui; l) per deiformem contemplationem; m) ad modum primorum principiorum; n) sine discursu; o) ex instinctu (divino); p) cognitio absoluta et simplex; q) quasi ex habitu.

captivating instances of the clear-obscure."[29] Because love is so closely bound up with what is individual—the concrete existent is its object—and because *individuum ineffabile est*, love defies complete conceptualization and expression. Despite this obscurity, however, there are certain fundamental principles which fall within the competence of the intellect. Among the first of these principles is the meaning of similitude as the cause of love.[30]

In a context of benevolent love—always the primary concern where charity is involved—the similitude, which is its cause, implies a mutual sharing of an identical form: "Any two things which possess the same form are somehow one in that form."[31] This common participation of the same form, whether substantial or accidental, creates a certain connaturality, a similarity, a "being one" in the same nature. Such connaturality is not caused by love; it is, rather, the cause of love. As the existential pre-requisite for love, it might be called ontological or antecedent connaturality. While this ontological connaturality remains constant, the act of love, by producing an affective union between the lover and the loved, adds to it an intentional perfection. Now recognized as a common sharing of the same nature and seen as the foundation for subsequent love, the prior connaturality is deepened but in another order. The *unio* and *mutua inhaesio* associated with love add a new dimension to the connatural roots of love, an affective or intentional dimension.[32] There are, therefore, two moments of connaturality, one

[29]"Dans la vie de l'esprit, *tout ce qui est relatif à l'amour*, dit St. Thomas (*Summa* I, q. 37, a. 1), *est particulièrement mystérieux et souvent innommé*, parce que l'intelligence connaît moins ce qui se trouve en une autre faculté que ce qui est en elle, et parce que l'amour *tend vers le bien*, qui est dans les choses et non dans l'esprit: cette tendance, comme tout ce qui reste encore indéterminé, n'est pas pleinement intelligible. Il y a là encore un clair-obscur des plus captivants." R. Garrigou-Lagrange, *Le sens du mystère dans le clair-obscur intellectuel* (Paris: Desclée de Brouwer, 1934), p. 17.

[30]Cf. *Summa* I-II, q. 27, a. 3.

[31]"Aliqui duo, quasi habentes unam formam, sunt quodammodo unum in forma illa." *Ibid.*, c.

[32]Cf. *Summa* I-II, q. 28, aa. 1 and 2.

ontological or antecedent, which is the cause of love; the other, intentional or consequent, which is its effect. As we shall see below, the intentional connaturality following upon love is the immediate source of affective knowledge.

b. In the Light of Being Loved

Although it may be true that love establishes a true connaturality between the lover and the loved, how could this have any influence in the intellectual order? In other words, is not the very phrase, affective knowledge, contradictory?

To understand the possibility of an affective influence at the cognitive level, the immediacy of intellect and will must first be grasped, for the transition from affectivity to knowledge demands that the will's act touch the intellect directly in some way. But is this true? Does the will directly touch the intellect? St. Thomas would say, yes, because "the act of the will is nothing other than a certain inclination following upon an apprehended form."[33] The will's act, as an inclination following upon a form apprehended by the intellect, is immediately present to the intellect. This intimacy is confirmed by the fact that both intellect and will are subjected in the soul as in the same substance. Consequently, what is in the will is experienced also by the intellect.[34] But does this experience of the affective act add anything to the conceptual knowledge in the intellect, which conditioned the will's act in the first place? Obviously, there can be no direct increase in conceptual comprehension, for the affective act, existential rather than essential, does not attain its object in its essence, which can be conceptualized, but in its existence, which is beyond conceptualization. However, as the will is drawn to the thing it loves, the goodness

---

[33]"Actus voluntatis nihil aliud est quam inclinatio quaedam consequens formam intellectam." *Summa* I, q. 87, a. 4, c.

[34]"Actum voluntatis (intellectus) percipit per redundantiam motus voluntatis in intellectum ex hoc quod colligantur in una essentia animae." *In III Sent.*, D. 23, q. 1, a. 2, 3m. Cf. also *Summa* I, q. 87, a. 4, ad 1: "Cum utrumque radicetur in una substantia animae, et unum sit quodammodo principium alterius, consequens est ut quod est in voluntate, sit etiam quodammodo in intellectu."

of the object, intentionally present in the intellect, is now experienced more intimately in its concrete attractiveness. The object is re-evaluated in the light of its being loved, as the abstract presentation made by the intellect is enriched, not conceptually or intentionally, but experientially.

In the light of being loved—this is the meaning of the now traditional phrase: "Affectus transit in conditionem obiecti."[35] The intellect experiences the object, connaturalized and made present in the will by love, and illumined by affectivity. The act of love becomes a formal medium, as the intellect judges the object, now seen in the light of love. While the obscurity regarding this affective knowledge remains, the possibility of its reality seems substantiated. Its ultimate basis: the unitive power of love.[36]

2. The Knowledge Born of Charity

In the supernatural order, where the natural primacy of the intellect is no longer operative, the possibility of affective knowledge becomes extremely important. The voluntary roots of faith and the supremacy of charity here below give an affective cast to the entire realm of the supernatural, a condition reflected in the highest intellectual perfection of all, the gift of wisdom.

Basing himself on the promise made by Our Lord at the Last Supper, St. Thomas speaks of a knowledge born of affectivity. He writes: "Through love for divine realities they are made manifest (to us), according to Jn. 14:21: 'If anyone love me, he shall be loved by my father, and I shall love him and shall

---

[35]John of St. Thomas, *Curs. Theol.*, In I-II, q. 68-70, Disp. 18, a. 4, no. 11 (Laval, no. 584). As explained recently, "the intellect first knows the goodness of the object in an abstract manner, in relation to the principles of practical knowledge. By reason of this, the goodness of the object is present to the will and can move it to act in the order of final causality. The intellect immediately knows the act of the will experimentally, and through it, the goodness of the object in a new and more intimate way." P. McCarroll, O.P., *The Gift of Wisdom and the Order of Justice according to St. Thomas* (Unpublished doctoral thesis, Angelicum, Rome, 1952), p. 82.

[36]"Amor est magis unitivus quam cognitio." *Summa* I-II, q. 28, a. 1, ad 3.

A theology of wisdom

manifest myself to him.' "[37] In other texts, St. Thomas, treating *ex professo* of the gift of wisdom, clearly designates its source as an affective connaturality or union with God. As one example:

> The wisdom that is a gift of the Holy Spirit renders right judgment of divine realities and of other things in the light of divine rules. This judgment is based in a certain connaturality or union with those divine realities, which, in turn is realized through charity. Therefore, the wisdom of which we speak presupposes charity.[38]

The affective union with God becomes the formal medium through which the individual in grace judges divine and created things, all in the light of God as the highest cause.[39] In a sense,

[37]"Ex ipsa enim divinorum affectione provenit manifestatio eorundem, secundum illud *Joan.* XIV, 21: 'Si quis diligit me diligetur a Patre meo, et ego diligam eum et manifestabo ei meipsum.' " *De Ver.*, q. 26, a. 3, 18m.

[38]"Sapientia quae est donum Spiritus Sancti facit rectitudinem iudicii circa res divinas, vel per regulas divinas de aliis, ex quadam connaturalitate sive unione ad divina. Quae quidem est per caritatem. Et ideo sapientia de qua loquimur praesupponit caritatem." *Summa* II-II, q. 45, a. 4, c. A more adequate presentation of wisdom's link with charity is found in article 2 of the same question: "Sapientia importat quandam rectitudinem iudicii secundum rationes divinas. Rectitudo iudicii potest contingere dupliciter: uno modo, secundum perfectum usum rationis; alio modo, propter connaturalitatem quandam ad ea de quibus iam est iudicandum. Sicut de his quae ad castitatem pertinent per rationis inquisitionem recte iudicat ille qui didicit scientiam moralem; sed per quandam connaturalitatem ad ipsa recte iudicat de eis ille qui habet habitum castitatis. Sic igitur circa res divinas ex rationis inquisitioni rectum iudicium habere pertinet ad sapientiam quae est virtus intellectualis: sed rectum iudicium habere de eis secundum quandam connaturalitatem ad ipsa pertinet ad sapientiam secundum quod donum est Spiritus Sancti: sicut Dionysius dicit in cap. 2 de *Div. Nom.*, quod Hierotheus est perfectus in divinis *non solum discens, sed et patiens divina.* Huiusmodi autem compassio sive connaturalitas ad res divinas fit per caritatem, quae quidem unit nos Deo, secundum illud *1 Cor.* 6:17: *Qui adhaeret Deo unus spiritus est.* Sic ergo sapientia quae est donum causam quidem habet in voluntate, scilicet caritatem; sed essentiam habet in intellectu, cuius actus est recte iudicare." Cf. also *In III Sent.*, D. 34, q. 1, a. 2, sol.; D. 35, q. 2, a. 1, sol. 3; a. 2, sol. 3; *In Phil.*, c. 1, lect. 2, no. 17; *Summa* II-II, q. 9, a. 2, ad 1; q. 60, a. 1, ad 2.

[39]"Ratio formalis sapientiae est procedere ex causis et rationibus divinis (quae sunt altissimae causae) ad indagandas veritates sive divinas sive creatas: *Spiritualis enim omnia judicat* (1 Cor. 2:15); sed tamen istae causae divinae et altissimae per quas procedit sapientia ad reddendam rationem non sunt notae quasi quidditative per sapientiae donum, sed quasi affective et mystice ex connaturalitate quadam et unione seu experientia interiori divinorum." John of St. Thomas, *Curs. Theol.*, In I-II, q. 68-70, Disp. 18, a. 4, no. 8 (Laval, no. 570).

the union of love plays a role analogous to that of an impossible species of the divine nature.[40] The experience of charity, under the special inspiration of the Holy Spirit, permits one to "taste and see that the Lord is sweet."[41]

This affective knowledge at the supernatural level is apparently limited to the higher mode proper to the gifts. Otherwise, their necessity would be compromised. The question, therefore, whether faith alone with charity could be the source of a supernatural knowledge through connaturality, without a special motion of the Holy Spirit, seems to demand a negative response.[42] Such a position, based as it is upon the Holy Spirit's identification with the realm of charity—"The charity of God is poured forth in our hearts by the Holy Spirit who has been given to us"[43]—safeguards the place of the Holy Spirit in the lives of the just. Always present in charity, he alone (by appropriation, of course) gives to it the perfection of becoming a light for the intellect.

While wisdom's formal light is affective—God is viewed in the light of being loved—it remains, nevertheless, essentially

[40]"C'est précisément le propre du don de sagesse d'user de l'*unio affectiva* propre à un tel amour (charité) déjà radicalement passif, et des effets de cette union, sous l'inspiration et l'illumination spéciale du Saint-Esprit, comme moyen de connaître, et d'élever, si l'on peut ainsi parler, la connaturalité amoureuse à jouer (comme l'essence divine elle-même dans la vision béatifique) un rôle analogue à celui qui jouerait une impossible spécies de la déité, et à procurer ainsi une expérience proprement dite de l'objet divin." Maritain, *Les degrés*, pp. 865-66.

[41]*Ps.* 33:7. Cf. the commentary of St. Thomas on this verse.

[42]This is also implied by St. Thomas, when he discusses the relation of the state of grace to the gift of wisdom in *Summa* II-II, q. 45, a. 5. Cf. Cajetan, *Commentaria in Summam Theologiae*, II-II, q. 45, a. 5. The well-known controversy between so-called acquired and infused contemplation, far too involved to be introduced here, concerns precisely this question. For the reasons already given, that is, the danger of compromising the necessity of the gifts and the immediate presence of the Holy Spirit in charity, the proponents of "acquired contemplation" seem to be mistaken. Although there is true acquired contemplation, most perfectly realized as the principal act of both metaphysical and theological wisdom, on the supernatural level there can be no *formally affective* contemplation, unless it be infused. No doubt, a certain acquired contemplation, not fully theological, is possible at the supernatural level, but at best it could involve only the initial and terminal affectivity discussed earlier, not the affectivity of charity as a formal light.

[43]*Rom.* 5:5.

intellectual. The experience of charity implies an illuminative inspiration of the Spirit under whose motion the "spiritual man judges all things."[44] The gift of wisdom involves judgment, though one founded upon an affective experience, and as a habit of judgment, it is an intellectual, not an affective, perfection.[45] This means that wisdom must be rooted in faith, the unique source of all supernatural judgment. The gift does not attain an object different from that of faith; only the mode of its knowledge is not the same.[46] This will be discussed more fully later, when wisdom is examined as perfective of faith.

The nature of wisdom, recognized as affective knowledge, finds its ultimate explanation in the perfection and primacy of charity. We have seen that charity, unlike faith, requires no medium in order to attain its object, for "the will attains its object immediately and in itself."[47] That immediacy of charity, going beyond the obscurity of faith, creates the possibility of an inspired judgment through affective experience.[48]

---

[44] *1 Cor.* 2:15.

[45] Cf. *Summa* II-II, q. 45, a. 2, c. This is in direct contrast to the statement made by Peghaire: "Il (le don de sagesse) sera donc reçu, et dans l'intelligence et dans la volonté." *Ratio et intellectus*, p. 295.

[46] "La sagesse mystique, goûtant et souffrant dans l'amour cela même que la foi atteint comme caché, nous fait juger et estimer de façon meilleure ce que nous connaissons par la foi, mais ne nous découvre aucun objet de connaissance que la foi atteindrait pas. Elle perfectionne la foi quant au mode de connaître, non quant à l'objet connu." Maritain, *Les degrés*, p. 524.

[47] "Voluntas feratur in ipsum objectum immediate et in se." John of St. Thomas, *Curs. Theol.*, In I-II, q. 68-70, Disp. 18, a. 4, no. 13 (Laval, no. 589). In the words of St. Thomas: "Actus voluntatis perficitur in hoc quod voluntas inclinatur ad ipsam rem prout in se est." *Summa* I, q. 82, a. 3, c.

[48] ". . . fides sua obscuritate attingit Deum secundum quandam distantiam ab ipso, quatenus fides est de non visis, charitas autem attingit Deum immediate in se, intime se uniens ei quod occultatur fide. Et sic licet fides regulet amorem et unionem ad Deum quatenus objectum proponit, tamen ex ista unione qua tangitur ab affectu Deus immediate eique unitur, movetur intellectus sicut a quadam experientia affectiva ad judicandum altiori modo de divinis quam illa obscuritas fidei patiatur, quia penetrat et cognoscit plus latere in rebus fidei quam fides manifestat, quia plus ibi amat et plus gustat in affectu, et ex illo plus quod cognoscit judicat altius de ipsis rebus divinis, innitens affectui experimentali (priusquam nudo testimonio credentis) cum instinctu Spiritus Sancti sic altiori modo certificantis et moventis intellectum." John of St. Thomas, *Ibid.*, no. 14 (Laval, nos. 590-91).

This is wisdom's nature. It remains for us to examine its primary act.

B. INFUSED WISDOM'S PRIMARY ACT: CONTEMPLATION

"The gift of wisdom leads to a certain divine and somehow explicit contemplation of the articles which faith holds obscurely according to a human mode."[49]

In the economy of the gifts the individual, possessing the Holy Spirit in charity, is moved by the divine motion on a plane above what is human. He is placed at a level consonant with the supernatural orientation of man. The ontological connaturality with God, realized in grace, is enriched by the intentional, affective connaturality of charity, in which wisdom's inspired judgment is given birth. Since this judgment is made primarily of charity's object, God as supreme good and ultimate final cause, it is immediately contemplative.

But to speak of the primary *act* of infused wisdom may be misleading. The gifts, unlike the virtues, are not perfections subject to the individual will. They dispose the soul for the motion of the Spirit "Who breathes where he will."[50] An act of the gift, therefore, is less active than passive; the initiative comes totally from without. And because of this element of passivity, it is called an experience.[51] The contemplation of wisdom lacks the conceptual clarity of metaphysical and theological contemplation—as formally affective, it is non-conceptual—but the immediacy of God, illumined by infused love, is truly experiential. The individual suffers the divine, according

---

[49]"Procedit sapientiae donum ad quandam deiformem contemplationem et quodammodo explicitam articulorum quos fides sub quodam modo involuto tenet secundum humanum modum." *In III Sent.*, D. 35, q. 2, a. 1, q1a. I, 1m.

[50]*Jn.* 3:8.

[51]"C'est bien là une expérience, si le mot expérience signifie la connaissance d'un objet comme présent, où l'âme souffre une action exercée par lui sur elle, et perçoit en raison de cette passion actuellement subie." Maritain, *Les degrés*, p. 521.

to the well-known phrase of the Pseudo-Dionysius: *patiens divina.*[52]

While this contemplative act proceeds from the gift of wisdom, faith and charity are necessarily present to make it possible. Mystical contemplation, another name applied to the act under discussion, "is produced at the same time by the intellect and by the will, by faith, by charity, and by wisdom: by faith, in regard to the essentially divine object; by charity, as to its formal medium; by the gift of wisdom, with regard to its experimental mode."[53] Three habits appear, therefore, as sources of infused contemplation in the subject: faith, which presents the object conceptually; charity, which unites subject to object affectively; and the gift, which remains the proximate principle of contemplation, itself, essentially an intellectual act.

1. Infused Contemplation and Finality

All wisdom necessarily involves a knowledge of highest cause, of God seen as principle and end of all things, identifying in himself goodness and truth.[54] Not a mere object, God is personal, infinitely intelligible, supremely lovable, recognized by the wise man—whether metaphysician, theologian, or individual in grace—as man's true ultimate end, criterion of all judgment and order. In a context of the gift, the contemplative contact with God is passive, supra-conceptual, quasi-experimental—all because its formal medium is the charity, "poured forth into our hearts by the Holy Spirit who has been given to us."[55] Yet,

[52]*De Divinis Nominibus*, c. 2; St. Thomas, *In De Div. Nom.*, c. 2, lect. 4, nos. 191-92.

[53]"Contemplation mystique . . . est produit à la fois par l'intelligence et par la volonté, par la foi, la charité, et la sagesse: par la foi quant à son objet essentiellement divin; par la charité quant à son moyen formel; par le don de sagesse quant à son mode expérimental." Maritain, *Les degrés*, p. 867. Cf. *Summa* II-II, q. 45, a. 1, ad 2: "Donum sapientiae praesupponit fidem"; and a. 2, c.: "Sapientia causam habet in voluntate, scilicet caritatem."

[54]St. Thomas affirms the analogy of wisdom and the application of Aristotle's wisdom concept to the gift in *Summa* II-II, q. 45, a. 1, c. Cf. also *In III Sent.*, D. 35, q. 2, a. 1, q1a. 2, sed contra.

[55]*Rom.* 5:5.

the gift's contemplation, viewing God in the light of his being
loved, remains engaged in judgment. St. Thomas writes:

> The gift of wisdom enjoys a perfection of knowledge attained
> through union with divine things, to which we are not united
> except by love—in the sense that he who adheres to God
> is one spirit with him (1 Cor. 6:17). Thus the Lord claimed
> to have revealed the secrets of his Father to the disciples
> because they were his friends (Jn. 15:15). The gift of wisdom,
> therefore, presupposes love as its principle and so involves
> affectivity. But it is essentially intellectual. For this reason,
> its act seems to be to contemplate both here and hereafter
> divine things loved and by them to judge other things not
> only speculatively but also practically—and this latter judgment
> depends upon an awareness of finality.[56]

The "divine things loved" represent a greater realization of
God as "the highest good, our ultimate end, the knowledge of
which makes a man truly wise."[57] His infinite goodness, seen
now in the light of affective connaturality, is appreciated more
deeply as ultimate final cause. Since, as we saw in the preceding
chapters, contemplation implies a knowledge not merely of
an object but of an object recognized as an end, this new
appreciation of God and finality gives to infused wisdom an
immediate orientation to contemplation. The contemplative judgment of the spiritually wise man orders everything in relation
to the ultimate final cause, God, whose goodness is now grasped
more perfectly in affective knowledge. The maxim, *sapientis
est ordinare*, finds here its ultimate contemplative realization on
earth, as the individual under the inspired motion of the Holy

[56]"Sapientiae donum eminentiam cognitionis habet, per quandam unionem
ad divina quibus non unimur nisi per amorem ut qui adhaeret Deo
sit unus spiritus (1 Cor. 6:17). Unde et Dominus, (Jn. 15:15), secreta
Patris se revelasse discipulis dicit, inquantum amici erant. Et ideo sapientiae
donum dilectionem quasi principium praesupponit, et sic in affectione
est. Sed quantum ad essentiam in cognitione est. Unde ipsius actus
videtur et hic et in futuro divina amata contemplari, et per ea de aliis
judicare non solum in speculativis, sed etiam in agendis, in quibus ex
fine judicium sumitur." *In III Sent.*, D. 35, q. 2, a. 1, sol. 3.

[57]". . . summum bonum, quod est ultimus finis per cuius cognitionem
homo dicitur vere sapiens." *Summa* II-II, q. 45, a. 1, ad 1.

Spirit and in the light of charity experienced becomes aware of God and all other things in their relation to him.

As the contemplative acts of metaphysics and theology represent relative participations of future happiness, so the act of infused wisdom, by which "man is united to those highest causes and transformed into their likeness,"[58] must also be a participation, temporary and imperfect though it be, of heaven's happiness.[59] The gift is not yet vision, for "the wisdom by which we now contemplate God does not touch God immediately in himself but rather the effects through which we now contemplate him."[60] And yet the illumination of the Holy Spirit makes possible a true affective knowledge of God, a knowledge without inference, which enjoys the immediacy of all affectivity; but it remains a knowledge of God only as imaged in his supernatural effects.[61]

Whether the object of the gift is referred to primarily as *res divinae*[62]—*causa altissima*[63]—*finis ultimus*[64]—*divina amata*[65]—or *rationes divinae*,[66] God is the center of wisdom's contemplation. He is generalized by the phrase, *divine things;* linked directly to wisdom by the characterization, *highest cause;* given causal primacy as *ultimate end;* made an affective object through the necessary association of finality and affectivity in the

[58]"Homo illis causis altissimis uniatur, transformatus in earum similitudinem." *In III Sent.*, D. 34, q. 1, a. 2, sol.

[59]"Actus sapientiae est quaedam inchoatio seu participatio futurae felicitatis." *Summa* I-II, q. 66, a. 5, ad 2.

[60]"Sapientia, qua nunc contemplamur Deum, non immediate respicit ipsum Deum, sed effectus ex quibus ipsum in praesenti contemplamur." *De Virt. in Comm.*, q. un., a. 12, 11m. Cf. the remarks of Maritain, *Les degrés*, p. 517, note 1 (cited below in part, note 110).

[61]"In a supernatural knowledge of which supernatural love is the formal medium, man can see these more perfect images of God, the gifts (wisdom and charity), and, in that vision, grasp without inference God himself there imaged. And by such a direct contact man truly possesses the Persons really present." F. Cunningham, O.P., *The Indwelling of the Trinity* (Dubuque: The Priory Press, 1955), p. 354.

[62]*Summa* II-II, q. 45, a. 4, c.

[63]*Ibid.*, a. 1, c.

[64]*Ibid.*, ad 1.

[65]*In III Sent.*, D. 35, q. 2, a. 1, sol. 3.

[66]*Summa* II-II, q. 45, a. 3, ad 3. The phrase appears as "divinas regulas" in the body of the article.

words, *divine things loved;* and seen, finally, as the rule of the practical order, when identified with *divine reasons.*

2. Infused Contemplation and Affectivity

In the discussion of metaphysics we saw that affectivity enters the picture only at the term of that natural wisdom, in the recognition of God as ultimate final cause of all things, and, therefore, as the metaphysician's own final end. In theology, affectivity comes not merely as an after-thought, accompanying the recognition of ultimate final cause, where God is viewed supernaturally as a Trinity of persons. It is true that the affective element in theology reaches here its perfection, yet it is already present, radically, at the very threshold of the supernatural, since "faith begins in affectivity."[67] This affective dimension in faith creates a germinal affectivity in theology, whose principles are provided by faith. Consequently, a greater degree of affectivity is present in theology than in metaphysics. In both these acquired wisdoms, however, the contemplative acts connote only initial and terminal affectivity; neither is formally affective. But the gift of wisdom, whose formal light is the connaturality caused by charity, is formally affective. It must involve greater affectivity, therefore, than either of the acquired wisdoms.

The contemplation of the spiritually wise man, while remaining essentially intellectual, views God through an affective medium. Under the inspiration of the Holy Spirit he contemplates God precisely as loved. There is, of course, also the initial and terminal affectivity common to all true contemplation, but here charity is present between these two affective moments, acting as a cognitive light. In this light the ultimate finality of divine goodness is experienced in a way impossible to merely conceptual knowledge, and wisdom's contemplative judgment is realized. The combination of these cognitive and affective elements is suggested in the following text of St. Thomas:

---

[67]"Inchoatio fidei est in affectione." *De Ver.*, q. 14, a. 2, 10m.

That knowledge from which love proceeds is alive in those fervent with divine love. It is a knowledge by which they know the divine goodness precisely as end and as superabundantly diffusing itself in them. Such knowledge indeed is not possessed perfectly by those who are not set on fire by the love of God.[68]

Not only is it true that the act of infused wisdom is to contemplate *divina amata*,[69] but the fact that divine things are loved provides the very content of the contemplation. Love becomes essential, and the first affective movement, discovered in faith, realizes its ultimate perfection here below, as it is crowned by the contemplative act of infused wisdom.[70]

3. *Infused Contemplation and Realism*

If it is true that the affective order always suggests greater realism than the intellectual order—the will attains its object as a whole and as it exists, while the intellect conceptualizes reality—then the affective dimension, so evident in the gift, gives to infused wisdom a realism impossible to lesser wisdoms. The goodness of God is known affectively, experienced through the medium of charity, and in the intimacy of that experience are present all the existential values associated with the will and its acts. Among the first of these is that the loved is made present in the lover. God, as contemplated in the light of being loved, is known as present. This is why, for St. Thomas, the presence of the Trinity in the soul in grace is formally constituted—with regard to its intellectual character and the cor-

---

[68]"Illa notitia ex qua procedit amor, viget in ferventibus divino amore, qua scilicet cognoscunt divinam bonitatem inquantum est finis, et inquantum est largissime in eos profluens sua beneficia; et talem notitiam perfecte non habent qui amori ipsius non accenduntur." *In I Sent.*, D. 15, q. 4, a. 2, 4m.

[69]*In III Sent.*, D. 35, q. 2, a. 1, sol. 3.

[70]"Nous pensons que c'est par cette première et essentielle dépendance où elle est de l'amour que, sur l'intervention d'autres vertus, et des Dons du Saint-Esprit, la foi se prête à cet épanouissement qu'est pour elle la connaissance mystique, expérimentale de Dieu-Trinité." Labourdette, "La théologie," pp. 14-15, note 1.

responding mission of the Word—by the gift of wisdom.[71] And the presence of God, as Father, Son, and Holy Spirit, loved in charity and known in wisdom, realizes for the individual in grace, however imperfectly and impermanently, his destiny as a rational creature. Nothing on earth could be more important than this gift of infused contemplation, realist and existential in both its form—as an experience—and its end—the attainment of God.

All this may seem a bit exalted in a context devoid of mention of great mystics. St. Thomas, however, sees no contradiction in such a position. Although he does admit higher levels of perfection within the order of the gifts—greater degrees of docility, for example, approaching complete passivity, with regard to the divine mover—nevertheless, he holds that this contemplation is meant for every Christian in the state of grace.[72] When referring to the contemplation characteristic of that state, he writes:

> Although everyone who is in the active life may not attain the perfect state of contemplation, nevertheless every Christian *in the state of grace* must participate in some contemplation, since the command is for all: "Be still and know that I am God" (Ps. 45:11).[73]

---

[71]Cf. *Summa* I, q. 43, a. 5, ad 2. See also R. Morency, S.J., *L'union de grâce selon St. Thomas* (Montréal: Les éditions de L'Immaculée Conception, 1950), pp. 197-206. Another writer remarks in this context: "The grace-gift of Wisdom, founded in supernatural Charity, gives man the power to know God as he is in himself in a quasi-experimental manner. The formal reason of the indwelling of the Father and the Son and the Holy Spirit is this gift of the Holy Spirit, which presupposes the supernatural habit of Charity and issues in supernatural love." Cunningham, *The Indwelling*, pp. 352-53.

[72]"Die Gaben und die mit ihnen verbundenen Erleuchtungen und Einsprechungen sind demnach als etwas Normales, grundsätzlich für alle Geltendes im Bereich des Gnadenslebens anzusehen, so selten sie auch im Christenleben in Erscheinung treten mögen." Utz, "Kommentar," p. 644.

[73]"Quamvis ad perfectum statum contemplationis non perveniat omnis qui in vita activa est, tamen omnis Christianus qui in statu salutis est oportet quod aliquid de contemplatione participet, cum praeceptum sit omnibus: *Vacate et videte quoniam ego sum Deus* (Psal. XLV, 11)." *In III Sent.*, D. 36, a. 3, 5m.

While later mystical writers have limited the notion of infused contemplation to only extremely high degrees of sanctity, this does not mean that it is completely foreign to less saintly souls who yet enjoy the effects of grace.[74] The gift of wisdom must bring with it its essential act, and although the actualization of what is potential in the gift as a habit in no way depends upon the individual, it seems unwarranted to hold that the gift remains forever habitual in certain souls. Here again, the necessity of the gifts would seem compromised.

In any case, the realism of infused wisdom's contemplation must mean ultimately a realism of arrival, of attainment. Raised to the supernatural order by grace, introduced to God in faith and committed to him affectively in charity, the human person attains God through infused contemplation and enjoys in the shadows of affective, experiential knowledge, a foretaste of eternal light.

C. INFUSED WISDOM AS SPECULATIVE AND PRACTICAL

To say that the gift of wisdom is not only speculative but also practical reflects an awareness, first of all, that God, as the primary object of wisdom, is the ultimate final cause of all human activity. This suggests, in turn, that the contemplation of God as end should introduce a consideration of him as the rule by which possible means are judged. The act of wisdom, says St. Thomas, is to contemplate divine things loved, "and by them to judge other things not only speculatively but also practically—the latter judgment depends upon an awareness of finality."[75] But this is not enough, taken alone, to justify the

---

[74]Writers who speak of infused contemplation only as the normal *term* of the life of grace must also give a restricted meaning to the phrase. Cf. Maritain, *Les degrés,* p. 512; also Garrigou-Lagrange, *Christian Perfection and Contemplation,* transl. (St. Louis: Herder, 1949), p. 420. If infused contemplation as the act of the gift of wisdom were only terminal, there would be no universal necessity for the gift.

[75]". . . et per ea de aliis judicare non solum in speculativis, sed etiam in agendis, in quibus ex fine judicium sumitur." *In III Sent.,* D. 35, q. 2, a. 1, sol. 3. "Superiores rationes quibus contemplandis sapientia

practical dimension in infused wisdom. By the same token, metaphysics would also be practical. What is more important is the more perfect participation in God's own knowledge, realized through the gift of wisdom. Like theology, infused wisdom is a *quaedam impressio divinae scientiae,* but, unlike theology, it is made possible through the instrumentality of charity, not of reason. Since God's knowledge is eminently both speculative and practical—in the identical intellectual act he knows both himself and what he creates—so, too, these created reflections of that divine knowledge share in their respective orders the eminent inclusion of speculative and practical values.

Although St. Thomas sometimes refers simply to a judgment given by wisdom regarding human acts,[76] he qualifies this considerably in texts where he points up explicitly wisdom's regulation of those acts.[77] This recalls the problem, discussed earlier, regarding the number, seven, as signifying precisely seven formally distinct habits. If wisdom actually *regulates* human activity—its profound involvement in the affective order suggests an existential immediacy not present in other intellectual perfections—why must there be a distinct gift of counsel? Unlike theology, whose practical judgments must be applied to the singular instance by a separate virtue of prudence, infused wisdom's more perfect, affective judgment of the divine goodness as one's ultimate end would seem to include an immediate awareness and acceptance of necessary means. Whatever be the true position, for the dialectical nature of the problem pre-

inhaeret, etiam operationum nostrarum regulae sunt. Unde secundum quod assumit eas ut regulas operabilium sic in praxim extenditur." *Ibid.,* a. 3, q1a. 2, 3m.

[76]*In III Sent.,* D. 34, q. 1, a. 2, sol.; a. 4, sol.; D. 35, q. 2, a. 1, sol. 3; *Summa* II-II, q. 45, a. 4, c.

[77]*In III Sent.,* D. 35, q. 2, a. 3, q1a. 2, 3m (cf. above, note 75); a. 4, sol. 2; *Summa* II-II, q. 45, a. 1, c.; a. 3, c. and ad 3; a. 6, ad 3. The judgment and actual direction appear side by side, when St. Thomas discusses wisdom's concern for "conspiciendis quidem, secundum quod divina in seipsis contemplatur; consulendis autem, secundum quod per divina *iudicat* de humanis, per divinas regulas *dirigens* actus humanos." *Summa* II-II, q. 45, a. 3, c.

cludes any final judgment, the ruling and directing of human acts proper to the gift become a second instance of wisdom's claim, *sapientis est ordinare*: "There is first in wisdom the *contemplation of divine things,* i.e., the vision of the principle, then the *direction of human acts* according to the divine rules."[78]

III. THE EFFECTS OF INFUSED WISDOM

In this final section several proper characteristics of infused wisdom shall be considered. Unlike the acquired wisdoms, both potential wholes whose various acts or functions form ordered constellations around the principal act of contemplation, the gift of wisdom embraces a plurality of effects, rather than different acts. Having already considered contemplation and the direction of human acts, it but remains to examine their effects. Since the inherent imperfection of the theological virtues in man makes the gifts necessary, our initial consideration will be of wisdom as it perfects the theological virtues. And because of wisdom's more immediate relation to charity and the primacy of affectivity in the supernatural order, the gift will be studied first as perfective of charity; secondly, as perfective of faith. Following this, wisdom's relation to the indwelling of the Trinity shall be noted briefly. Finally, the supreme effect of wisdom's practical dimension shall be presented, before its radical incompleteness, as being only *quasi*-experimental, concludes the chapter.

A. INFUSED WISDOM AS PERFECTIVE OF CHARITY

When the gifts are said to perfect the theological virtues,[79] this does not mean that wisdom, for example, is more perfect

---

[78]"Ad sapientiam per prius pertinet contemplatio divinorum, quae est visio principii; et posterius dirigere actus humanos secundum rationes divinas." *Summa* II-II, q. 45, a. 3, ad 3.

[79]"Omnia dona ad perfectionem theologicarum virtutum ordinantur sicut ad finem." *Summa* II-II, q. 9, a. 1, ad 3. "Dona perficiunt virtutes elevando eas supra modum humanum." *De Caritate*, q. un., a. 2, 17m. Cf. also *Summa* I-II, q. 68, a. 2.

in itself than faith or charity.[80] It means, rather, that the theological virtues with the gifts are more perfect than the same virtues without them.[81] But this, too, must be qualified. Faith and charity are not perfected by wisdom in the same way. While faith is perfected intrinsically—that is, the conceptualization of revealed truth is directly affected—wisdom gives to charity only an extrinsic perfection. This will be clarified below. Basically, the reason is that the will in itself does not connote the imperfection necessarily implied in human intellection: "Here below we love God in his essence; we do not see him in his essence."[82] If wisdom gives to faith a higher mode, it presents charity only with a more adequate judgment of the divine goodness, a judgment which is extrinsic to charity itself.

With the immediacy characteristic of the affective order wisdom—always within faith—adds to the intentional grasp of God's goodness a dimension at once supra-conceptual, experiential, and far more realistic. Concrete and individual, this experience of infinite goodness is more engaging than the abstract conception presented by faith. And because the divine goodness is the proper object of charity, this greater appreciation of that goodness provides charity with a more adequate intellectual basis for its act of love. "Both human intellection and human love are directed by wisdom."[83] Here the direction is operative at the summit of human affectivity, where charity unites man to God. The affective judgment of wisdom, therefore, makes up for the disproportion existing between faith and the needs of

[80]The superiority of the theological virtues rests upon the immediacy of their relationship to God. God himself is their proper object. The gifts, however, do not unite man to God directly, but rather dispose him to receive the divine motion. Cf. *Summa* I-II, q. 68, a. 8, c.

[81]". . . l'axe de la vie spirituelle se trouve vraiment dans les vertus théologales, supérieures aux dons, mais qui reçoivent de ces derniers une perfection nouvelle." Garrigou-Lagrange, "L'axe de la vie spirituelle et son unité," *Revue thomiste*, 43 (1937), p. 360. Cf. also Maritain, *Les degrés*, p. 863 (cited below, note 94).

[82]"In statu viae Deum per essentiam amamus, non videmus." *In III Sent.*, D. 34, q. 1, a. 1, 5m.

[83]"Per sapientiam dirigitur et hominis intellectus et hominis affectus." *Summa* I-II, q. 68, a. 4, ad 5.

charity, which requires a greater appreciation of divine excellence than faith alone gives to it.[84]

If wisdom provides charity with a more perfect condition for its exercise—"a good cannot be loved unless it is known"[85]— charity, in its turn, deepens through affective experience the contact of wisdom. In a framework of reciprocal causality, dispositive and formal, wisdom conditions charity, while charity provides the light for wisdom. As an affective knowledge whose object is "the divine goodness seen as end and as generously diffusing itself in us"[86] the gift of wisdom serves and is served by the highest gift of him whose very name is *Donum*,[87] the gift of Father and Son to one another. As above, charity enjoys an absolute primacy in making this knowledge possible, for "such knowledge is not possessed perfectly by those who are not set on fire by the love of God."[88]

B. INFUSED WISDOM AS PERFECTIVE OF FAITH

As remarked earlier, wisdom must presuppose faith.[89] Its entire orientation looks to the foundation provided by faith, for the

[84]Cf. Gardeil, *La structure de l'âme et l'expérience mystique* (Paris: Gabalda, 1927) II, 203-06. To say that charity has a strict need for a more perfect judgment than the one presented in faith, is not completely true. Such an argument (cf., for example, McCarroll, *The Gift of Wisdom,* pp. 173-80) seems to beg the question. As John of St. Thomas remarks: "Licet non proponatur sibi res (in fide) ut est in se, sed sub testimonio extrinseco, tamen hoc in illo velamine proponitur quod plus latet de re quam cognoscatur et manifestatur; et illud plus quod latet etiam desiderat voluntas, illique unitur affectus, quod nescit proponere intellectus." *Curs. Theol.,* In I-II, q. 68-70, Disp. 18, a. 4, no. 13 (Laval, no. 589).
[85]"Bonum non potest amari nisi cognitum." *Summa* I-II, q. 27, a. 2, c.
[86]". . . divinam bonitatem inquantum est finis et inquantum est largissime in eos profluens sua beneficia," *In I Sent.,* D. 15, q. 4, a. 2, 4m. Cf. also *Summa* II-II, q. 8, a. 5, c. and ad 2, where St. Thomas speaks of the "aestimationem rectam de ultimo fine," as provided by the gift of understanding. According to the position we have chosen, in which infused wisdom embraces also understanding, this correct evaluation of ultimate finality is made by the gift of wisdom.
[87]*Summa* I, q. 38, aa. 1 and 2.
[88]*In I Sent.,* D. 15, q. 4, a. 2, 4m. Cf. *supra,* note 68.
[89]"(Sapientia) differt a fide. Nam fides assentit veritati divinae secundum seipsam; sed iudicium quod est secundum veritatem divinam pertinet ad donum sapientiae. Et ideo donum sapientiae praesupponit fidem; quia unusquisque bene iudicat quae cognoscit . . ." *Summa* II-II, q. 45, a. 1, ad 2.

intellectual gifts "are ordered to the supernatural knowledge which is in us by faith."[90] This necessity of faith, as a prerequisite for the gift, stems from the very nature of affective knowledge; for without an intentional union of subject and object, an affective union would be impossible.[91] God must be known before he can be loved. Faith must precede charity, whose affective light can illumine only an object already held by the intellect. The ultimate *raison d'être* of the gift of wisdom is not the absence of an intellectual grasp of the divine object but the imperfection of faith's contact with that object—God is known in obscurity, for "we see now through a mirror, in an obscure manner."[92] As St. Thomas remarks, wisdom involves a divine and somehow explicit contemplation of the articles, which faith holds obscurely and according to a human mode.[93] Infused wisdom, therefore, is grounded in faith, and though in itself less perfect, it adds a perfection otherwise impossible to faith alone.[94] But how, precisely, does wisdom perfect faith?

1. The nature of faith demands conceptualization of revealed truths—they are known according to a human mode, through the medium of concepts abstracted from creatures. If this conceptual knowledge is to be perfected, that is, if the obscurity of conceptual representation of the divine is to be transcended, it cannot be realized by the addition of more concepts. The inadequacy of faith is rooted in its very nature as conceptual. Moreover, since the source of possible perfection, the gift of

[90]". . . ordinantur ad supernaturalem cognitionem quae in nobis per fidem fundatur." *Summa* II-II, q. 8, a. 6, c.

[91]Cf. M. D. Roland-Gosselin, O.P., "De la connaissance affective," *Revue des sciences philosophiques et théologiques*, 27 (1938), p. 23.

[92]*1 Cor.* 13:12. Cf. the analysis of Pauline doctrine on faith, in Dupont, *Gnosis*, chap 3: "Dans un miroir, en énigme," pp. 105-48.

[93]*In III Sent.*, D. 35, q. 2, a. 1, q1a. 1, 1m.

[94]". . . le don de sagesse est inférieur aux vertus théologales, il n'a pas pour objet spécificateur Dieu lui-même *secundum suam propriam quidditatem*. Il est donc, tant que nous pérégrinons ici-bas, au service de la foi. Comment dès lors pourrait-il aller plus loin que la foi, 'réussir là où la foi échoue,' et nous conduire à l'expérience de l'union en abstrayant de la foi . . .? C'est la foi perfectionnée par les dons qui réussit là, où la foi toute seule échoue." Maritain, *Les degrés*, p. 863.

wisdom, is essentially affective knowledge, it is necessarily non-conceptual.[95] But in what way might a non-conceptual knowledge improve upon what is conceived by faith? In a word, only by transcending the concepts of faith *negatively*. By making more apparent the radical impossibility of human concepts to express the divine nature, the experience of infused wisdom makes faith more profoundly meaningful. Paradoxically, faith is perfected by emphasis placed upon its imperfection. This negative transcendence of the conceptual order of faith is remarkably expressed by Jacques Maritain, as he writes—the text is beyond translation:

> Pour devenir sagesse et contemplation, la connaissance de foi devra, sous une grâce divine d'inspiration et d'illumination . . . faire cesser progressivement ce *de loin*, cet *à distance*, c'est-à-dire, devenir expérimentale et procéder apophatiquement (négativement), en se délivrant du mode limité des concepts, non par une connaissance intellectuelle qui transcenderait le oui û et le non, mais par une passion des choses divines, qui goute et touche par le non la profondeur infinie du oui.[96]

2. In the preceding chapters we saw that both metaphysical and theological knowledge culminate in mystery, the mystery of God as ultimately unknowable. But this final completion of knowledge in ignorance is even more impressive, one might say, even more essential, at the level of the gifts. The supra-conceptual character of infused wisdom actually means the negation of conceptual values. It is true, the affirmations of faith are not destroyed, but transcended in this process of negation.[97] And yet, with the content of its concepts more negated than affirmed, the mind is left in ultimate, though not total, ignorance. It seems a remarkable testimony to the poetic irony of the human situation, that the highest knowledge of all

[95] All affective knowledge is knowledge of the individual, concrete existent, which is beyond conceptualization: "Individuum ineffabile est."
[96] *Les degrés*, p. 484.
[97] Cf. Journet, *Introduction*, p. 44: "Les négations, on le voit, ont ici pour fin, non de détruire les affirmations, mais d'enchérir sur elles."

terminates in ignorance: "God remains in the shadows of our ignorance within which, as Denis says, we are best united to him here below; and this is the darkness in which God is said to dwell."[98] But as is evident in the paradox, expressed above in the text of Maritain, it is an ignorance, whose negative darkness contacts a world of infinite affirmation, the affirmation of eternal light.[99]

3. In the absence of conceptualization, the knowledge proper to the gift of wisdom is necessarily incommunicable. Because of the immediacy implied in all affective knowledge, the experience of God in wisdom is beyond conception and, therefore, beyond communicability. Words, the sole means of communication, can only signify concepts, and without concepts the *res* remains incommunicable. In the order of *vox* (spoken word)— *verbum* (mental word)—*res* (thing), there is no other possible way for the *vox* to signify the *res*, except by first signifying the *verbum* or concept. Since here there is no *verbum*, there can be no *vox*. Communication is impossible. To speak of mystical experience as ineffable, therefore, is not only poetic expression; it is the literal evaluation of an experience beyond conception and communication.

4. Stemming from this incommunicability, inherent in the nature of infused wisdom, is the qualified subordination of that wisdom to theology—"qualified" because the gift remains always objectively superior to theology. When mystical experience is expressed in human language, however, it becomes answerable to theology. Actually, there is a relationship of mutual influence between the two. While theology controls the attempt made at conceptual expression by infused wisdom, the gift, in its turn,

---

[98]"(Deus) remanet in quadam tenebra ignorantiae, secundum quam ignorantiam, quantum ad statum viae pertinet, optime Deo conjungimur, ut dicit Dionysius, et haec est quaedam caligo, in qua Deus habitare dicitur." *In I Sent.*, D. 8, q. 1, a. 1, 4m.

[99]The subjective state of the individual, wrapped in this veil of ignorance, is described by Journet, as he writes: "Et alors son seul dessein est de *se taire*, car elle sent jusqu'à la souffrance la radicale impuissance des mots et des concepts à exprimer la plénitude divine." *Introduction*, p. 29.

illumines theology, in much the same way as faith might illumine philosophy.[100] But, as a contemporary writer explains, when referring to theology's judgment of infused wisdom:

> Without doubt, it is not for the theologian without love to judge by himself a wisdom which surpasses him; it is the Church, who enlists theological science to judge the mystics, because scientific wisdom alone is able to judge the conformity of mystical phenomena with the principles of faith. This judgment according to the human mode is connatural to her status as the Church militant.[101]

Infused wisdom as perfective of faith implies first, therefore, the negative transcendence of faith's concepts. From a conceptual point of view, this is but a euphemistic expression for ignorance. But the ignorance of the divine mystery is not total—as essential, not existential, it is ignorance of what God is, not of what he is not. With the lack of conceptualization, infused wisdom is incommunicable, and when it seeks to be heard in

[100]". . . dans les énoncés communicables par où le langage humain traduit l'expérience mystique . . . la sagesse mystique est contrôlable par la théologie. Le théologien juge ainsi le contemplatif non en tant même que contemplatif, mais en tant que le contemplatif descend dans le champ de l'expression conceptuelle et de la communication rationelle. Un astronome peut juger de même un philosophe qui parle astronomie. Mais de soi la sagesse mystique est supérieure à la sagesse théologique, et c'est le spirituel qui, non pas sans doute dans l'ordre de la doctrine, mais dans celui de l'expérience et de la vie, juge le théologien spéculatif." Maritain, *Les degrés,* pp. 24-25, note 3.

[101]"Sans doute, ce n'est pas au théologien sans amour à juger par lui-même d'une sagesse qui le dépasse, mais l'Eglise se sert avec profit de la science théologique pour contrôler les spirituels, parce que la sagesse scientifique seule peut rendre *raison* de la conformité des phénomènes mystiques avec les principes de la foi. Ce jugement à mode humain est le plus connaturel à son objet d'Eglise militante." Philipon, "La théologie comme science," p. 415. According to John of St. Thomas: ". . . licet secundum se altius sit (donum sapientiae) quam sapientia theologica nostris actibus hic acquisita, tamen quoad nos propter imperfectum modum participandi dona Spiritus Sancti, praesertim quae ad illustrationem intellectus pertinent quae in hac vita subordinantur fidei . . . oportet quod sapientia donum et judicium theologiae mysticae examinetur et innitatur judicio sapientiae acquisitae et theologiae scholasticae . . . ideo necesse est quod isti actus doni sapientiae, ut nobis certificentur, regulentur per sapientiam acquisitam, tum propter subordinationem doni ad virtutem fidei quae est altior donis et certius veritates continet; tum propter majorem evidentiam in illationibus sapientiae acquisitae." *Curs. Theol.,* In II-II, De Spe, Disp. 6, a. 1, no. 6 (Vives, VII, 376).

the world of men, it must answer to the conceptual wisdom of theology. All this is suggested in wisdom's relation to faith.

C. INFUSED WISDOM AND THE INDWELLING OF THE TRINITY

"As the known is in the knower and the loved is in the lover" is the way St. Thomas describes the indwelling of God in the souls of the just.[102] The union is one of operation, actual or habitual, in which the individual enjoys the supernatural power of knowing and loving God, already present in the soul through efficient causality.[103] At first thought, one might be inclined to see faith and charity as the principles of this union. However, faith can exist without charity, and the special presence of God in grace requires a knowing principle with a necessary orientation to love—"and as the loved is in the lover." There must be an essential link with charity.[104] It is a living faith, therefore, as perfected by the gift of wisdom, which is the intellectual source of the Trinitarian inhabitation. The indwelling of the Divine Persons in souls in grace is formally constituted by charity and the infused wisdom to which it gives birth.[105]

---

[102]". . . sicut cognitum in cognoscente et amatum in amante." *Summa* I, q. 43, a. 3, c. Cf. also *In I Sent.*, D. 14, q. 2, a. 2, 3m; D. 37, q. 1, a. 2, sol.; *In III Sent.*, D. 10, q. 3, a. 1, sol. 1; *De Pot.*, q. 9, a. 9, c.; *De Ver.*, q. 29, a. 1, c.; *De rationibus fidei*, c. 6; *Summa* I, q. 8, a. 3, c. and ad 4; III, q. 2, a. 10, c.; q. 6, a. 6, ad 1; *In Joan.*, c. 2, lect. 3, no. 2; *In I Cor.*, c. 3, lect. 3.

[103]Cf. the discussion of operational union in Morency, *L'union de grâce*, pp. 161-241.

[104]The theology of the divine missions which form the background for the indwelling of the Trinity, is based upon charity, by which or in which the Holy Spirit is given to us. Without charity, there is no mission of the Spirit, and, consequently, no mission of the Word. St. Thomas explains: "Non qualiscumque cognitio sufficit ad rationem missionis, sed solum illa quae accipitur ex aliquo dono appropriato personae, per quod efficitur in nobis conjunctio ad Deum, secundum modum proprium illius personae, scilicet per amorem, quando Spiritus Sanctus datur. Unde cognitio ista est quasi experimentalis." *In I Sent.*, D. 14, q. 2, a. 2, 3m. Cf. also *Summa* I, q. 43, a. 5, ad 2.

[105]". . . we know the gifts of the Trinity by experiencing them; and by their gifts we know, we experience the Divine Persons themselves . . . in the experimental knowledge, which Wisdom gives birth to, whose cause and formal medium is divine Charity, the formal explanation of the Trinity in the souls of the just is found." Cunningham, *The Indwelling*, p. 202.

A theology of wisdom

God is present "as the known is in the knower," but as one known through the experience of love, as the object of the gift of wisdom.

D. INFUSED WISDOM AND PEACE

The three properties discussed above flow from wisdom, seen primarily as speculative; even the experiential judgment of ultimate final cause, whereby wisdom conditions charity, touches the practical order only from the top. Perfective of both faith and charity, wisdom unites them in itself to form the basis for the Trinitarian indwelling. In this section, we look briefly at a proper effect of wisdom's practical dimension, peace, as it is influenced by infused wisdom.

St. Thomas characterizes peace as a formal effect of charity.[106] In associating peace with wisdom, therefore, that relationship of peace with charity must be qualified. "To have peace," writes the Common Doctor, "is proper to charity, but to establish peace is proper to an ordering wisdom."[107] Since peace, according to the traditional definition of St. Augustine, is *tranquillitas ordinis*—the tranquillity of order—a principle of order is necessarily a principle of peace. But *sapientis est ordinare*. The judgments of order and hierarchy in regard to the appetitive life of the individual, as well as in regard to the communal life among men, find their source in wisdom. And what is more important, not only the judgment, but the actual ordering according to that judgment stems from infused wisdom. For this reason, although both the acquired wisdoms of metaphysics and theology can be genuine sources of peace for the individual, strictly speaking, peace is the proper effect of infused wisdom. This is the final realization of the maxim, *sapientis est ordinare*. Wisdom—Order—Peace.

---

[106]*Summa* II-II, q. 29, a. 3.

[107]"Caritatis est habere pacem sed facere pacem est sapientiae ordinantis." *Summa* II-II, q. 45, a. 6, ad 1.

E. THE INCOMPLETENESS OF INFUSED WISDOM

The desire at which metaphysics terminates, to know God from within, is partially satisfied by the more intimate knowledge of faith and theology. But because faith and its rational development in theology remain conceptual, the finite limitations of the concepts condition a desire to touch God more immediately, no longer through the medium of concepts but in himself. While this may have been hoped for in the gift of wisdom, it is not realized. It is true, God is known differently, supra-conceptually and more concretely, in the experiential knowledge of the gift, but the immediacy involved is not between the intellect and God, but rather, between the intellect and the act of love which unites the individual to God. It is an experience directly of charity,[108] and only indirectly of God.[109] That is why St. Thomas calls the knowledge *quasi*-experimental.[110] Al-

---

[108] " 'Spiritus reddit testimonium quod sumus filii Dei' . . . per effectum amoris filialis, quem in nobis facit." *In Rom.*, c. 8, lect. 3, no. 645.

[109] "Sapientia, qua nunc contemplamur Deum, non immediate respicit ipsum Deum, sed effectus ex quibus ipsum in praesenti contemplamur." *De Virt. in Comm.*, q. un., a. 12, 11m. Cf. also *In I Sent.*, D. 16, q. 1, a. 2, sol.; *De Ver.*, q. 18, a. 1, 4m.

[110] *In I Sent.*, D. 14, q. 2, a. 2, 3m. Maritain precises: "Ce que nous appelons ici *objectum quo*, ce n'est pas la charité ni la sagesse prises comme habitus, ce sont des passions actuellement subies par l'âme, des effets actuels servant de medium actuel de connaissance sous l'illumination du Saint-Esprit. Ainsi Dieu est connu encore *par ses effets* . . ." *Les degrés*, p. 517, note 1. A recent study on the subject of experimental knowledge concludes: ". . . while the possibility of interpreting our *quasi experimentalis cognitio* of the divine persons as immediate or supra-discursive knowledge cannot absolutely be ruled out, we have found no evidence that postulates such an interpretation.

"Accordingly, all that is clear from our study of St. Thomas is that *experimental or quasi-experimental knowledge of the divine persons is the knowledge that is accompanied by the affective experience of love and spiritual taste.*" J. Dedek, *Experimental Knowledge of the Indwelling Trinity: An Historical Study of the Doctrine of St. Thomas* (Mundelein, Illinois: St. Mary of the Lake Seminary, 1958), p. 147.

First of all, there is evidence, at least by way of an argument from analogy, that the cognitive mode of the gift is non-discursive. When referring to the gifts of *intellectus* and *scientia*, St. Thomas speaks, on the one hand, of an apprehension "sine discursu" (*In III Sent.*, D. 35, q. 2, a. 2, sol. 1) and on the other, of the similarity of the gift to the divine knowledge which "non est discursiva vel ratiocinativa." (*Summa* II-II, q. 9, a. 1, ad 1)

But what is more disconcerting is what Fr. Patfoort calls "la formule vague, plate et non compromettante à laquelle aboutit malheureusement

though infused wisdom, therefore, connotes the immediacy proper to all affective knowledge, it is not yet vision. The gift must also terminate in desire.

*   *   *

While the ascending degrees of wisdom illumine the darkness in which infinite light plunges the human mind, the obscurity is never completely overcome. From metaphysics, which remains forever outside the divine, to theology, which enters only conceptually that world of inaccessible light, to infused wisdom, which enjoys the experiential overtones of affectivity, God remains essentially unknown.[111] At the highest reaches of human intellectual perfection knowledge culminates in ignorance, and there remains but the desire for vision.

ce travail par ailleurs si suggestif." (*Bulletin thomiste,* 10 [1957-59], p. 543) If affectivity merely accompanies the knowledge of wisdom without acting in some manner as its formal light, why postulate a cognitive gift in the first place. Faith would suffice.

[111]When speaking of this ultimate ignorance, however, "il faut distinguer *l'obscurité inférieure* qui vient de l'incohérence et de l'absurdité, et *l'obscurité supérieure,* qui vient d'une trop grande lumière pour les faibles yeux de notre esprit." Garrigou-Lagrange, *Le sens du mystère,* p. 127. This higher obscurity explains the ultimate unknowability of God.

SUMMARY

In a field of study as vast as that suggested by the word, wisdom, to present conclusions too all-embracing would seem out of place. Wisdom is filled with too many overtones of historical and doctrinal significance to permit being exhaustively examined in a work such as this. The chapters that have gone before make no claim to be exhaustive. However, they do contain several leading thoughts which, while not meant to pose as last words on the subject, are not without real foundation. It may be well to resume them here.

To begin with, the historical roots of the Thomistic notion of wisdom are undeniably Aristotelian. While St. Thomas was undoubtedly influenced by the sapiential texts of the Old Testament and by the refinements added by Christian Revelation, as well as by the wisdom doctrine of St. Augustine, his conception is based predominantly upon the thought of Aristotle. The commanding idea of knowledge of highest causes, hardly a legacy of sacred scripture or of St. Augustine, is everywhere apparent in the Thomistic texts. Yet what is more important than the Aristotelian influence in St. Thomas is his conception of wisdom in diverse realizations. Metaphysics, theology, and the gift of wisdom are three distinct realizations of an analogous intellectual perfection—this is the unique contribution of St. Thomas. The purpose of the present study has been to present these three wisdoms in synthesis, in comparative confrontation. Regarding each wisdom certain conclusions have been drawn, certain positions taken, but they are too numerous to be restated individually here. What shall be resumed are the ideas that touch directly upon wisdom in synthesis.

141

A *theology of wisdom*

First of all, the relationship between wisdom and contemplation is one between an intellectual habit and its principal or primary act. All wisdom implies a knowledge of God as ultimate final cause, which becomes the basis for the contemplative judgment of order in reality. Ultimately, that act, as expressed by St. Thomas, is to contemplate divine things loved—*divina amata contemplari*. While St. Thomas uses the phrase explicitly only in reference to the gift, in the analogy of wisdom it is applicable to the acquired wisdoms also, for supreme goodness cannot help but evoke an affective response. In wisdom's object supreme intelligibility is identified with supreme desirability—*prima veritas* with *summum bonum*—here is the source of wisdom's union with love. To contemplate divine things loved—this is the act of wisdom *par excellence* . . .

Secondly, the element of affectivity is found in ascending degrees among the three wisdoms. Present only at the term of metaphysics, where the individual confronts God as his own ultimate final cause, affectivity enters theology in faith, to be fully realized in the charity which crowns theological contemplation. In the gift of wisdom the formal light of the intellectual experience is affective—God is known in the light of being loved. Wisdom, viewed not phenomenologically but according to its own nature, cannot be separated from its affective dimension. This is the basis for the personal involvement implied by wisdom, an evidence of its profound realism . . .

Thirdly, an attempt has been made to give precision to the maxim, *sapientis est ordinare*. Most important, of course, is its realization in the contemplative judgment of each wisdom, as God is viewed with all things ranged hierarchically in reference to him. Further, in metaphysics and theology the wise man orders his own principles as well as the sciences inferior to his wisdom, and in theology and the gift there is the practical ordering, at least remotely, of human acts to their proper end. A final instance of the maxim is evident as infused wisdom effects the tranquillity of order we know as peace. *Sapientis est ordinare* . . .

Fourthly, the world of wisdom, paradoxically, is one of ultimate ignorance—*cognoscimus Deum tamquam ignotum*—we know God as one unknown. Yet, the ignorance of the wise man is preferable to all other knowledge, for though it may be ignorance of what God is, it is true knowledge of what he is not. This least knowledge of God, man's end and happiness, infinitely surpasses the most comprehensive knowledge of something other than God. But in this higher world of affirmation in negation there is an ultimate incompleteness, where a lower wisdom opens upon a higher one, where each wisdom terminates in desire. The desire is that of all created wisdom for a knowledge no longer of reflections but of the reality—a longing to possess Uncreated Wisdom in the vision of God himself.

Finally, the analysis of wisdom in its created realizations has been a work of theology, exercising one of its functions as wisdom. The argument presented in chapter three, emphasizing theology's sapiential character and all that that implies deserves being recalled here—it is the final summary thought demanding restatement. A theology of wisdom makes sense only because theology is wisdom.

There are other things that could have been said regarding the theology of wisdom. Other approaches could have been made to the study, another order followed in its presentation, and what has actually been written can claim little more than to have introduced a profound subject. But if the work does nothing more than suggest the reality and true significance of the three created wisdoms, above all, their contemplative realism, it will have served its purpose.

The author wishes to close with words first written by St. Thomas, as he finished his exposition of the *De Divinis Nominibus*. They are repeated here with greater reason: "Et nos, post expositionem dictorum beati Thomae, longe ab eius intellectu deficientes, corrigi de non recte dictis postulamus."

BIBLIOGRAPHY

I. WORKS OF ST. THOMAS

Opera Omnia, edit. Leonina, Romae, 1882 sqq.

Opera Omnia, edit. Parmensis, Parmae, 1852-73.

Scriptum Super Libros Sententiarum, edit. Mandonnet-Moos, Parisiis: Lethielleux, 1929 sqq., 4 vols.

Quaestiones Disputatae, edit. Marietti, Taurini, 1949, 2 vols.

Quaestiones Quodlibetales, edit. Marietti, Taurini, 1949.

In VIII Libros Physicorum Aristotelis Expositio, edit. Marietti, Taurini, 1954.

In XII Libros Metaphysicorum Aristotelis Expositio, edit. Marietti, Taurini, 1950.

In X Libros Ethicorum Aristotelis ad Nicomachum Expositio, edit. Marietti, Taurini, 1949.

Opuscula Theologica, edit. Marietti, Taurini, 1954, 2 vols.

Opuscula Philosophica, edit. Marietti, Taurini, 1954.

In Librum Boethii de Trinitate Quaestiones Quinta et Sexta, edit. Wyser, Fribourg: St. Paul, 1948.

In Librum Beati Dionysii De Divinis Nominibus Expositio, edit. Marietti, Taurini, 1950.

Super Evangelium S. Matthaei Lectura, edit. Marietti, Taurini, 1951.

Super Evangelium S. Ioannis Lectura, edit. Marietti, Taurini, 1952.

Super Epistolas S. Pauli Lectura, edit. Marietti, Taurini, 1953, 2 vols.

II. BOOKS

ARISTOTLE, *Opera omnia. Graece et Latina.* Parisiis: Firmin-Didot, 1848-87, 5 vols.

———— *The Works of Aristotle.* Edited by W. D. Ross. Oxford: Clarendon Press, 1908-31, 11 vols.

BAUMGARTNER, W. *Israëlitische und altorientalische Weisheit.* Sammlung Gemeinverständlicher Vorträge, 166. Tübingen, 1933.

BEUMER, J., S.J. *Theologie als Glaubensverständnis.* Würzburg: Echter, 1953.

CAJETAN, THOMAS DE VIO, *Commentaria in summam theologiae S. Thomae Aquinatis.* Edit. Leonina. Romae, 1888-1906.

CAYRE, F., A.A. *La contemplation augustinienne.* Bruges-Paris: Desclée et Brouwer, 1954.

CHENU, M. D., O.P. *Une école de théologie: Le Saulchoir.* Etiolle (S et O): Le Saulchoir, 1937.

———— *La théologie au douzième siècle.* Paris: Vrin, 1957.

———— *La théologie comme science au XIIIe siècle.* 3ième édition. Bibliothèque thomiste, 33. Paris: Vrin, 1957.

COLLINS, J., *The Lure of Wisdom.* Aquinas Lecture, 1962. Milwaukee: Marquette University Press, 1962.

CONTENSON, V., O.P. *Theologia mentis et cordis.* Coloniae Agrippinae: Metternich, 1687.

CUNNINGHAM, F., O.P. *The Indwelling of the Trinity.* Dubuque: The Priory Press, 1955.

DE KONINCK, C. *Ego Sapientia: La sagesse qui est Marie.* Québec: Laval-Fides, 1943.

DEDEK, J. F., *Experimental Knowledge of the Indwelling Trinity: An Historical Study of the Doctrine of St. Thomas.* Mundelein, Illinois: St. Mary of the Lake Seminary, 1958.

DEL PRADO, N., O.P. *De veritate fundamentali philosophiae christianae.* Fribourg: S. Paul, 1911.

DONLAN, T., O.P. *Theology and Education.* Dubuque: W. C. Brown Co., 1952.

DUESBERG, H., O.S.B. *Les scribes inspirés.* Introduction aux livres sapientiaux de la Bible. Paris: Desclée de Brouwer, 1939.

DUPONT, J., O.S.B. *Gnosis. La connaissance religieuse dans les épitres de Saint Paul.* Paris: Desclée de Brouwer, 1949.

FESTUGIERE, A. J. *Contemplation et vie contemplative selon Platon.* Paris: Vrin, 1936.

GAGNEBET, R., O.P. *De natura theologiae eiusque methodo secundum Sanctum Thomam.* Romae: Angelicum, 1950-52, 2 vols.

GARDEIL, A., O.P. *Le donné révélé*. Paris: Les éditions du Cerf, 1932.

———— *La structure de l'âme et l'expérience mystique*. Paris: Gabalda, 1927, 2 vols.

GARDEIL, H. D., O.P. *Initiation à la philosophie de St. Thomas d'Aquin*. IV, la métaphysique. Paris: Les éditions du Cerf, 1952.

GARRIGOU-LAGRANGE, R., O.P. *Christian Perfection and Contemplation*. Translation by Sr. M. T. Doyle, O.P. St. Louis: Herder, 1949.

———— *De revelatione*. 5ª editio. Rome: Desclée et Socii, 1950.

———— *Le sens du mystère et le clair-obscur intellectuel*. Paris: Desclée de Brouwer, 1934.

GILSON, E. *History of Christian Philosophy in the Middle Ages*. London: Sheed & Ward, 1955.

———— *Introduction à l'étude de Saint Augustin*. Paris: Vrin, 1943.

———— *La philosophie au moyen âge*. 2ième édition. Paris: Payot, 1944.

———— *Le thomisme*. Paris: Vrin, 1944.

———— *Wisdom and Love in Saint Thomas Aquinas*. Aquinas Lecture, 1951. Milwaukee: Marquette University Press, 1951.

GLUTZ, M., C.P. *The Manner of Demonstrating in Natural Philosophy*. St. Meinrad: Abbey Press, 1956.

GRABMANN, M. *Die theologische Erkenntnis- und Einleitungslehre des heiligen Thomas von Aquin auf Grund seiner Schrift In Boethium de Trinitate*. Thomistische Studien, Band IV. Freiburg Schweiz: Paulusverlag, 1948.

———— *Die Werke des hl. Thomas von Aquin, Eine literar-historische Untersuchung und Einführung*. 3e Auflage. Beiträge zur Geschichte der Philosophie des Mittelalters. Bd. XXII, Heft 1-2. Münster in W., 1949.

The Great Ideas—A Syntopicon of Great Books of the Western World. Edited by M. J. Adler. London: Encyclopaedia Britannica, 1952.

HEATH, T., O.P. *Aristotelian Influence in Thomistic Wisdom: a Comparative Study*. Washington: Catholic University Press, 1956.

JOHN OF ST. THOMAS, O.P. *Cursus philosophicus*. Editio Reiser. Taurini, 1933-37, 3 vols.

————— *Cursus theologicus.* Editio Solesmes. Paris, Tournai, Rome: Desclée et Socii, 1931 sqq.

————— *Cursus theologicus.* Editio Vives. Parisiis, 1883-86, 10 vols.

————— *In primam-secundae—de donis Spiritus Sancti.* Collectio Lavallensis. Québec, 1948.

JORET, F. D., O.P. *La contemplation mystique d'après Saint Thomas d'Aquin.* 2ième édition. Paris: Desclée de Brouwer, 1927.

JOURNET, C. *Connaissance et inconnaissance de Dieu.* Paris: Egloff, 1943.

————— *Introduction à la théologie.* Paris: Desclée de Brouwer, 1947.

KOELLIN, K., O.P. *Expositio commentaria in primam-secundae S. Thomae Aquinatis.* Venetiis, 1589.

LOTTIN, O., O.S.B. *Psychologie et morale aux XIIe et XIIIe siècles.* Louvain: Abbaye de Mont César, 1942-54, 4 vols.

McCARROLL, P., O.P. *The Gift of Wisdom and the Order of Justice according to St. Thomas.* Unpublished doctoral thesis. Rome: Angelicum, 1952.

MARCEL, G., *The Decline of Wisdom.* New York: Philosophical Library, 1955.

MARIN-SOLA, F., O.P. *L'évolution homogène du dogme catholique.* Fribourg: St. Paul, 1924, 2 vols.

MARITAIN, J. *Distinguer pour unir ou Les degrés du savoir.* Paris: Desclée de Brouwer, 1932.

————— *Science et sagesse.* Paris: Labergerie, 1936.

MARROU, H. I. *Saint Augustin et la fin de la culture antique.* Bibliothèque des Ecoles Françaises d'Athènes et de Rome. Paris: Boccard, 1938 ("Retractatio"—1949).

MORENCY, R., S.J. *L'union de grâce selon St. Thomas.* Studia Collegii Maximi Immaculatae Conceptionis, VIII. Montréal: L'Immaculée Conception, 1950.

MURPHY, R. E., O. CARM. *Seven Books of Wisdom.* Milwaukee: Bruce, 1960.

O'KEEFE, D. L. *Theology and Contemplation according to St. Thomas Aquinas.* Rome: Catholic Book Agency, 1952.

PEGHAIRE, J., C.S.Sp. *Intellectus et ratio selon St. Thomas d'Aquin.* Paris: Vrin, 1936.

PETRIN, J., O.M.I. *Connaissance spéculative et connaissance pratique.* Ottawa: Editions de l'Université d'Ottawa, 1948.

PHILIPPE, M. D., O.P. *Initiation à la philosophie d'Aristote.* Paris: La Colombe, 1956.

PIEPER, J. *Glück und Kontemplation.* München: Kösel-Verlag, 1957.

————— *Leisure the Basis of Culture.* Translation by A. Dru. London: Faber & Faber Ltd., 1952.

PRAT, F., S.J. *La théologie de St. Paul.* Vol. I. 10ième édition. Paris: Beauchesne, 1912.

ROUSSELOT, P., S.J. *L'intellectualisme de St. Thomas,* 3ième édition. Paris: Beauchesne, 1936.

ROY, L., S.J. *Lumière et sagesse.* Studia Collegii Maximi Immaculatae Conceptionis, VI. Montréal: L'Immaculée Conception, 1948.

SCHEEBEN, M. J., *The Mysteries of Christianity.* Translation by C. Vollert, S.J. St. Louis: Herder, 1946.

SCHUTZ, L., *Thomas-Lexikon.* Paderborn: Schöningh, 1895. New York: Ungar, 1957.

SMITH, V. E., *The School Examined—Its Aim and Content.* Milwaukee: Bruce, 1960.

VACANT, J. *Etudes théologiques sur les Constitutions du Concile du Vatican.* Paris: Delhomme Briguet, 1895.

VAN ACKEREN, G. F., S.J. *Sacra Doctrina—The Subject of the First Question of the Summa Theologica of St. Thomas Aquinas.* Rome: Catholic Book Agency, 1952.

WALLACE, W. A., O.P. *The Role of Demonstration in Moral Theology.* Washington: Thomist Press, 1962.

WHITE, V., O.P. *God the Unknown and Other Essays.* New York: Harper & Bros., 1956.

WILLIAMS, C., O.P. *De multiplici virtutum forma.* Rome: Angelicum, 1954.

Wisdom in Israël and in the Ancient Near East. Supplement to *Vetus Testamentum.* Edited by M. Noth and D. W. Thomas. Leiden: E. J. Brill, 1955.

WYSER, P., O.P. *Theologie als Wissenschaft.* Ein Beitrag zur theologischen Erkenntnislehre. Salzburg & Leipzig: Pustet, 1938.

III. Articles

ALLO, E. B., O.P. "Sagesse et Pneuma dans la première épitre aux Corinthiens," *Revue biblique,* 43 (1934) 321-46.

ALONSO, J. M., C.M.F. "La teologia como ciencia," *Revista española de teologia*, 4 (1944) 611-34; 5 (1945) 3-38, 433-50, 529-60.

BEUMER, J., S.J. "Conclusionstheologie," *Zeitschrift für katholische Theologie*, 63 (1939) 360-65.

———— "Thomas von Aquin zum Wesen der Theologie," *Scholastik*, 30 (1955) 195-214.

BOTTE, B., O.S.B. "La sagesse dans les livres sapientiaux," *Revue des sciences philosophiques et théologiques*, 19 (1930) 83-94.

BOYER, C., S.J. "Qu'est-ce que la théologie," *Gregorianum*, 21 (1940) 255-66.

BRETON, S., "Logique et théologie," *Revue des sciences philosophiques et théologiques*, 44 (1960) 409-40.

BROWNE, M., O.P. "Il metodo della teologia," *Sapienza*, 7 (1954) 5-16.

CAYRE, F., A.A. "Introduction générale," *Oeuvres de St. Augustin*, vol. I. (Paris: Desclée de Brouwer, 1949), pp. 46-99.

———— "La notion de sagesse chez St. Augustin," *L'Année théologique*, 4 (1943) 433-56.

CHENU, M. D., O.P. "Les philosophes dans la philosophie chrétienne médiévale," *Revue des sciences philosophiques et théologiques*, 26 (1937) 27-40.

———— "Position de la théologie," *Revue des sciences philosophiques et théologiques*, 24 (1935) 232-57.

———— "La théologie comme science au XIIIe siècle," *Archives d'histoire doctrinale et littéraire du moyen âge*, 2 (1927) 31-71.

CONGAR, Y., O.P. "Sur la théologie," *Bulletin thomiste*, 5 (1937-39) 490-505.

———— "Théologie," *Dictionnaire de théologie catholique*, T. XV, col. 346-502.

DAFFARA, M. "La teologia come scienza nella Somma teologica di S. Tommaso," *Sapienza*, 1 (1948) 12-22.

DE ANDREA, M., O.P. "Soggetto e oggetto della metafisica secondo S. Tommaso," *Angelicum*, 27 (1950) 165-195.

DE BOER, P. A., "The Counsellor," *Wisdom in Israël* (q. v.), pp. 42-71.

DE FINANCE, J. "La ΣΟΦΙΑ chez S. Paul," *Recherches des sciences religieuses*, 25 (1935) 385-417.

DEMAN, T., O.P. "Composantes de la théologie," *Revue des sciences philosophiques et théologiques*, 28 (1939) 386-434.

DOLAN, S. E., F.S.C. "Resolution and Composition in Speculative and Practical Discourse," *Laval théologique et philosophique*, 6 (1950) 9-62.

FEUILLET, A., P.S.S. "Jésus et la sagesse divine après les évangiles synoptiques," *Revue biblique*, 62 (1955) 161-96.

FOREST, A. "Le réalisme de la volonté," *Revue thomiste*, 46 (1946) 457-76.

GAGNEBET, R., O.P. "Dieu sujet de la théologie selon Saint Thomas d'Aquin," *Analecta gregoriana*, 68 (1954) 41-55.

――――― "La nature de la théologie spéculative," *Revue thomiste*, 44 (1938) 1-39, 213-55, 645-74.

――――― "Le problème actuel de la théologie et la science aristotélicienne d'après un ouvrage récent," *Divus Thomas Piacenza*, 20 (1943) 237-70.

――――― "St. Thomas constructeur de la science théologique," *Angelicum*, 27 (1950) 303-06.

GARDEIL, A., O.P. "Dons du Saint-Esprit," *Dictionnaire de théologie catholique*, T. IV, col. 1728-81.

GARRIGOU-LAGRANGE, R., O.P. "L'axe de la vie spirituelle et son unité," *Revue thomiste*, 43 (1937) 347-60.

――――― "Le clair-obscur de la sainte Trinité," *Revue thomiste*, 45 (1939) 647-64.

――――― "Science et sagesse," *Revue thomiste*, 41 (1936) 630-34.

――――― "La structure de l'âme et l'expérience mystique," *Revue des sciences philosophiques et théologiques*, 40 (1956) 652-56.

――――― "La théologie et la vie de la foi," *Revue thomiste*, 40 (1935) 492-514.

GEIGER, L. B., O.P. "Abstraction et séparation d'après St. Thomas," *Revue des sciences philosophiques et théologiques*, 31 (1947) 3-40.

GERMAIN, P., C.S.C. "La théologie de saint Thomas d'Aquin, science de la foi," *Revue de l'université d'Ottawa*, 28 (1958) 156*-84*.

GILSON, E. "La sagesse et le temps," *Lumière et vie*, 1 (1951) 77-92.

GLUTZ, M., C.P. "The Formal Subject of Metaphysics," *Thomist*, 19 (1956) 59-74.

GRABMANN, M. "De theologia ut scientia argumentativa," *Angelicum*, 14 (1937) 39-60.

HAYEN, A., S.J. "La théologie aux XIIe, XIIIe et XXe siècles," *Nouvelle revue théologique,* 79 (1957) 1009-28; 80 (1958) 113-32.

HIRSCHBERGER, J. "Quod sit officium sapientis," *Philosophisches Jahrbuch,* 53 (1940) 30-44.

KANE, W. H., O.P. "Abstraction and the Distinction of the Sciences," *Thomist,* 17 (1954) 43-68.

————— "Introduction to Metaphysics," *Thomist,* 20 (1957) 121-42.

————— "The Nature and Extent of Philosophy of Nature," *Thomist,* 7 (1944) 204-32.

————— "The Subject of Metaphysics," *Thomist,* 18 (1955) 503-21.

KLUBERTANZ, G., S.J. "Being and God according to contemporary Scholastics," *Modern Schoolman,* 32 (1954-55) 1-17.

LABOURDETTE, M., O.P. "Savoir spéculatif et savoir pratique," *Revue thomiste,* 44 (1939) 564-69.

————— "La théologic science de la foi," *Revue thomiste,* 46 (1946) 5-44.

————— "La vie théologale selon S. Thomas—affection dans la foi," *Revue thomiste,* 60 (1960) 364-80.

LECLERCQ, J., O.S.B. "La théologie comme science d'après la littérature quodlibétique," *Recherches de théologie ancienne et médiévale,* 11 (1939) 351-74.

LENZ, J. "Thomistische Philosophie als Lebensweisheit," *Pastor bonus* (Trier), 49 (1939-40) 323-37.

LINDBLOM, J. "Wisdom in the Old Testament Prophets," *Wisdom in Israël,* (q.v.), pp. 192-204.

LONERGAN, B., S.J. "Theology and Understanding," *Gregorianum,* 35 (1954) 630-48.

LOSSKY, V. "Eléments de théologie négative chez Saint Augustin," *Augustinus Magister,* (Congrès international Augustinien, Paris: Etudes Augustiniennes 1954), I, 475-81.

————— "La théologie négative dans la doctrine de Denys l'Aréopagite," *Revue des sciences philosophiques et théologiques,* 28 (1939) 204-21.

MARITAIN, J. "L'humanisme de Saint Thomas d'Aquin," *Medieval Studies,* 3 (1941) 174-84.

————— "Science et sagesse," *Nova et vetera,* 9 (1934) 389-407.

MOTTE, A., O.P. "Théodicée et théologie chez St. Thomas d'Aquin," *Revue des sciences philosophiques et théologiques,* 26 (1937) 5-26.

MOWINCKEL, S., "Psalms and Wisdom," *Wisdom in Israël* (q.v.), pp. 205-24.

MUNIZ, F., O.P. "De diversis muneribus sacrae theologiae secundum doctrinam S. Thomae," *Angelicum,* 24 (1947) 93-123.

NICOLAS, J.-H., O.P. "L'intuition de l'être et le premier principe," *Revue thomiste,* 47 (1947) 113-34.

OWENS, J., C.Ss.R. "A Note on the Approach to Thomistic Metaphysics," *New Scholasticism,* 28 (1954) 454-76.

PAISSAC, H., O.P. "Théologie, science de Dieu," *Lumière et vie,* 1 (1951) 33-56.

PATFOORT, A., O.P. "Review of DEDEK" (q.v.), *Bulletin thomiste,* 10 (1957-59) 539-43.

PHILBIN, W. J. "The Intellect's Part in Charity," *Irish Theological Quarterly,* 18 (1951) 303-21.

PHILIPON, M.-M., O.P. "Les dons du Saint-Esprit," *Revue thomiste,* 59 (1959) 451-83; 61 (1961) 241-54.

——— "La théologie science suprême de la vie humaine," *Revue thomiste,* 18 (1935) 387-421.

PHILIPPE, M. D., O.P. "Nature de l'acte de contemplation philosophique dans la perspective des principes d'Aristote," *Revue thomiste,* 49 (1949) 525-41.

——— "La sagesse selon Aristote," *Nova et vetera,* 20 (1945) 325-74.

PHILIPPE, P., O.P. "La contemplation au XIIIe siècle," *Dictionnaire de spiritualité,* T. II, col. 1966-88.

PHILIPPE, T., O.P. "Contemplation métaphysique et mystère de la création," *Revue des sciences philosophiques et théologiques,* 23 (1934) 345-58.

——— "L'intelligence mystère de lumière," *Revue des sciences philosophiques et théologiques,* 24 (1935) 434-61.

——— "Spéculation métaphysique et contemplation chrétienne," *Angelicum,* 14 (1937) 223-63.

PORTALIE, E., "Augustin," *Dictionnaire de théologie catholique,* T. I, col. 2268-2472.

A *theology of wisdom*

PORTEOUS, N. W., "Royal Wisdom," *Wisdom in Israël*, (q.v.), pp. 247-61.

ROLAND-GOSSELIN, M. D., O.P. "De la connaissance affective," *Revue des sciences philosophiques et théologiques*, 27 (1938) 5-26.

SMITH, V. E., "Wisdom and Science," *Proceedings of the American Catholic Philosophical Association*, 30 (1956) 3-15.

SPICQ, C., O.P. "La vertu de prudence dans l'ancien Testament," *Revue biblique*, 42 (1933) 187-210.

TASCON, T., O.P. "Note sur la place du don de sagesse dans la théologie morale thomiste," *Revue thomiste*, 35 (1930) 415-25.

THONNARD, F. J., A.A. "Science et sagesse dans la cité de Dieu," (Estudios sobre la "Ciudad de Dios," I) *La Ciudad de Dios*, 167 (1954) 511-24.

UTZ, F., O.P. "Kommentar in I-II, q. 68," *Die deutsche Thomas-Aufgabe: Summa Theologica*, Bd. XI. (Salzburg: Pustet, 1940), pp. 630-51.

VANDEN-BROUKE, F., O.S.B. "Le divorce entre théologie et mystique, ses origines," *Nouvelle revue théologique*, 72 (1950) 372-89.

———— "Notes sur la théologie mystique de Saint Thomas d'Aquin," *Ephemerides theologicae lovaniensis*, 27 (1951) 483-92.

VAN IMSCHOOT, P. "Sagesse et esprit dans l'ancien testament," *Revue biblique*, 47 (1938) 23-49.

XIBERTA, B., O.C. "De cooperatione voluntatis in cognitione," *Divus Thomas Piacenza*, 41 (1938) 494-507.

INDEX OF THOMISTIC TEXTS

This listing contains only the more important texts. Page numbers are given in parentheses.

Index of thomistic texts

156

Index of thomistic texts

GENERAL INDEX

This index contains references to specific persons and subjects. See also notes at head of entries for THOMAS AQUINAS and WISDOM.

General index

Epistemology, 37
    see also Knowledge
Eternal life, 17
Existence: mystery of being, 56, 58
Existentialists, 13

Faith
    affectivity, 61, 87, 125
    Augustine, 14
    concepts and, 61, 133, 139
    contemplatively incomplete, 81
    inchoative wisdom, 20n, 62
    infused contemplation, 122
    inquietude, 64
    knowledge, 82, 104
    living, 15, 92, 137
    love and the will, 87
    love preceded by, 133
    negative transcendence, 134
    object, 60f, 120
    perfected by wisdom, 131ff
    reason and charity, 63
    reason and theology, 76-77
    revelation and, 61, 97
    speculative intellect, 90
    spiritual growth, 88n
    supernatural knowledge, 60, 119
    supernatural virtue, 60
    theology and, 64ff, 86, 92
    understanding, 63ff
    Vatican Council on, 60, 64
    vision the end of, 65
    wisdom, 12, 20
Festugière, A. J., 3n
Final cause; finality
    Finis est causa causarum, 42, 84
    infused contemplation and, 122-23
    metaphysical contemplation and, 41, 56
    order and, 42, 83-84
    practical judgment, 128
    theological contemplation and, 83ff
First philosophy, *see* Metaphysics
First principles, 4, 37, 50ff, 95
    principle of contradiction, 52
Form: love and, 115

162

Theology
    affectivity, 125
    "conclusion-theology," 74, 80
    conclusions, 70
    conclusions of other sciences, 102
    contemplation as primary act, 81ff
    defensive function, 95
    definition (Muniz), 80n
    faith and, 86, 92
    faith and philosophy, 84
    functions of theological wisdom, 94ff
    gift of wisdom and, 135
    glory and justification of, 89n
    God as subject of, 78
    history in, 68-69
    holiness and, 91
    incompleteness of theological wisdom, 104
    metaphysics and wisdom, 79-80
    nature of, 66
    objective light, 75
    other sciences and, 101
    other sciences as handmaids, 103
    perfection of, 92
    positive and speculative, 68
    practical, 92
    primary act, 81ff
    primary object, 67
    principles, 94, 102
    purpose, 81
    rational techniques, 67
    reason and faith, 76-77
    sapiential character, 143
    as science, 69
    science of, 66
    science of salvation, 69
    scientific or demonstrative function, 97
    speculative as primary, 90
    speculative or practical, 19, 89ff
    spiritual life, 93-94
    as wisdom, 67ff
Theology and philosophy
    ends compared, 101
    methodology, 100
    mixing water and wine, 66, 103
    reason and faith, 65

General index